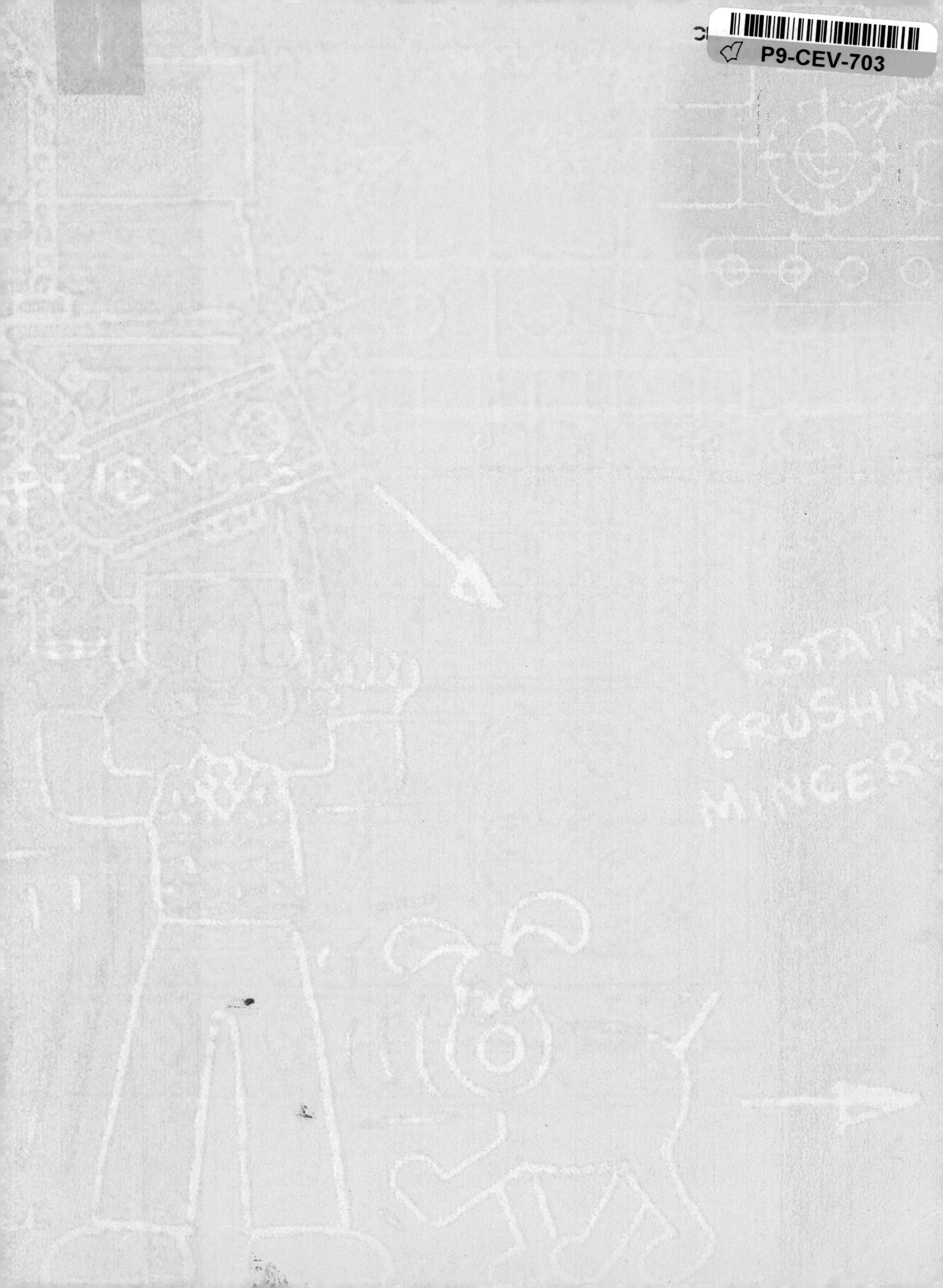
ROTATIN
CRUSHIN
MINCER

Aardman
presents

Wallace & Gromit ™

The Whippet Vanishes

Titan Books

Wallace & Gromit™
The Whippet Vanishes

HB ISBN 1 84023 497 0
PB ISBN 1 84023 498 9

Published by Titan Books,
a division of Titan Publishing Group Ltd.
144 Southwark St
London SE1 0UP
In association with Aardman Animation Ltd.

Grateful thanks and salutations to Dick Hansom and Rachael Carpenter
at Aardman Animations, and David Barraclough, Oz Browne,
Bob Kelly, Angie Thomas, Steve White and Katy Wild at Titan Books.

A CIP catalogue record for this title is available from the British Library.

Hardback edition: March 2004
Paperback edition: September 2004

1 3 5 7 9 10 8 6 4 2

Printed in Italy.

What did you think of this book? We love to hear
from our readers. Please email us at:
readerfeedback@titanemail.com, or write to us at
the above address. You can also visit us at
www.titanbooks.com

Aardman
presents

Wallace & Gromit ™

The Whippet Vanishes

Original story by Simon Furman and Ian Rimmer

Written by Ian Rimmer

Drawn by Jimmy Hansen

Coloured by John Burns

Lettered by Richard Starkings

Designed by Caroline Grimshaw

Edited by Simon Furman & Nick Jones

Wallace and Gromit created by Nick Park

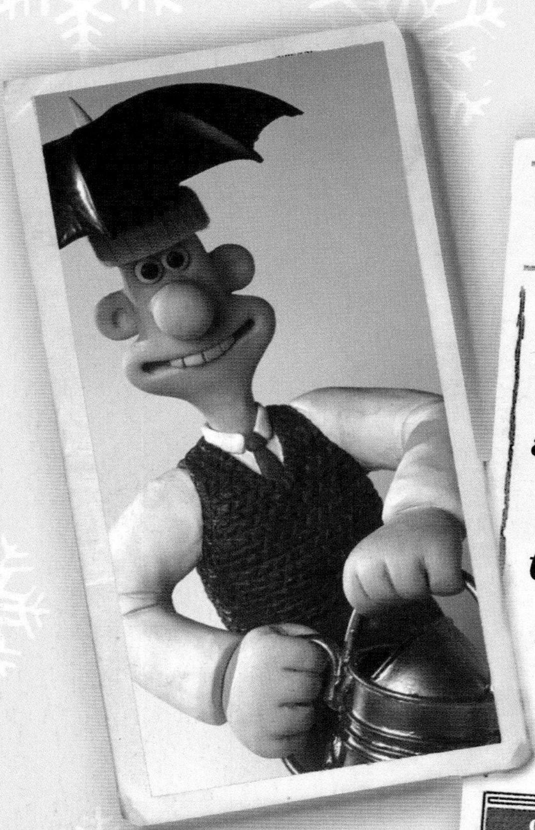

WALLACE

No. 1

Part-time inventor, amateur soft-boiled detective. No case too big, no clue too small, no solution too outrageous!

Issued by
CRACKING CONFECTIONERY
LONDON - - - ENGLAND
PRINTED IN ENGLAND

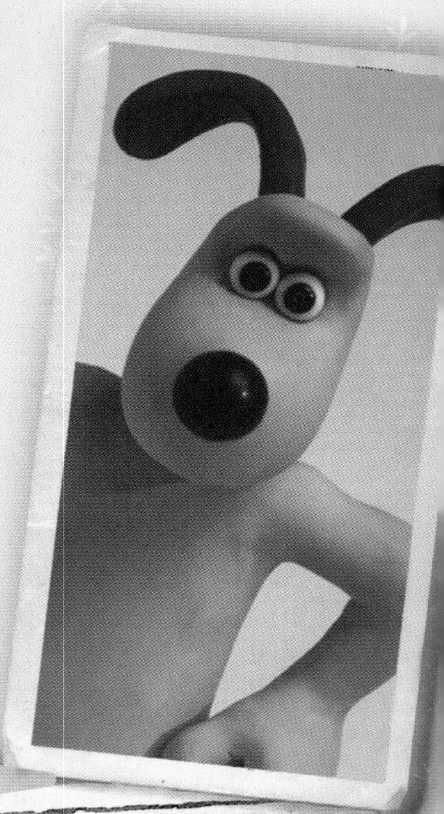

GROMIT

No. 2

Long-suffering companion, but the real brains of the outfit. Great at sniffing out trouble. Leads a dog's life.

Issued by
CRACKING CONFECTIONERY
LONDON - - - ENGLAND
PRINTED IN ENGLAND

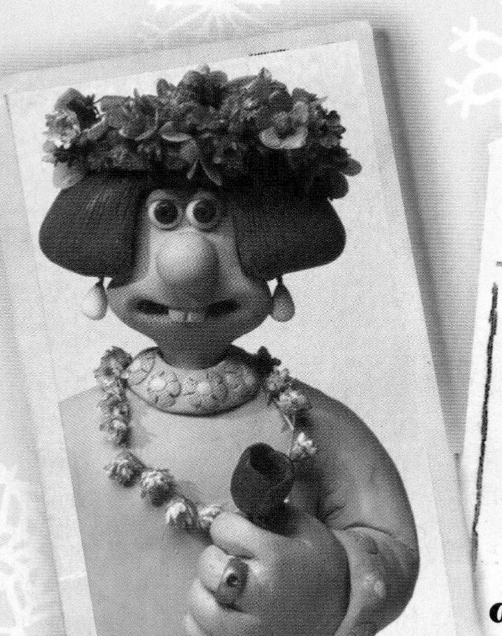

WENDOLENE

No. 3

Owner of town's Wool Shop and Wallace's would-be moll, although doesn't like cheese. Does like knitting and tea.

Issued by
CRACKING CONFECTIONERY
LONDON - - - ENGLAND
PRINTED IN ENGLAND

SHAUN

No. 4

The big sheep.
Lousy detective.
Will eat clues. Brain
largely replaced by
seemingly
bottomless
stomach.

Issued by
CRACKING CONFECTIONERY
LONDON - - - ENGLAND
PRINTED IN ENGLAND

PRESTON

No. 5

Former robot
'heavy' for sheep-
rustler. Ended up
eating lead and lots
of other metal
when crushed in
own machine.

Issued by
CRACKING CONFECTIONERY
LONDON - - - ENGLAND
PRINTED IN ENGLAND

FEATHERS McGRAW

No. 6

Identikit penguin
and criminal
mastermind. Tried
to feather nest with
stolen diamond but
got busted. Now in
the cooler.

Issued by
CRACKING CONFECTIONERY
LONDON - - - ENGLAND
PRINTED IN ENGLAND

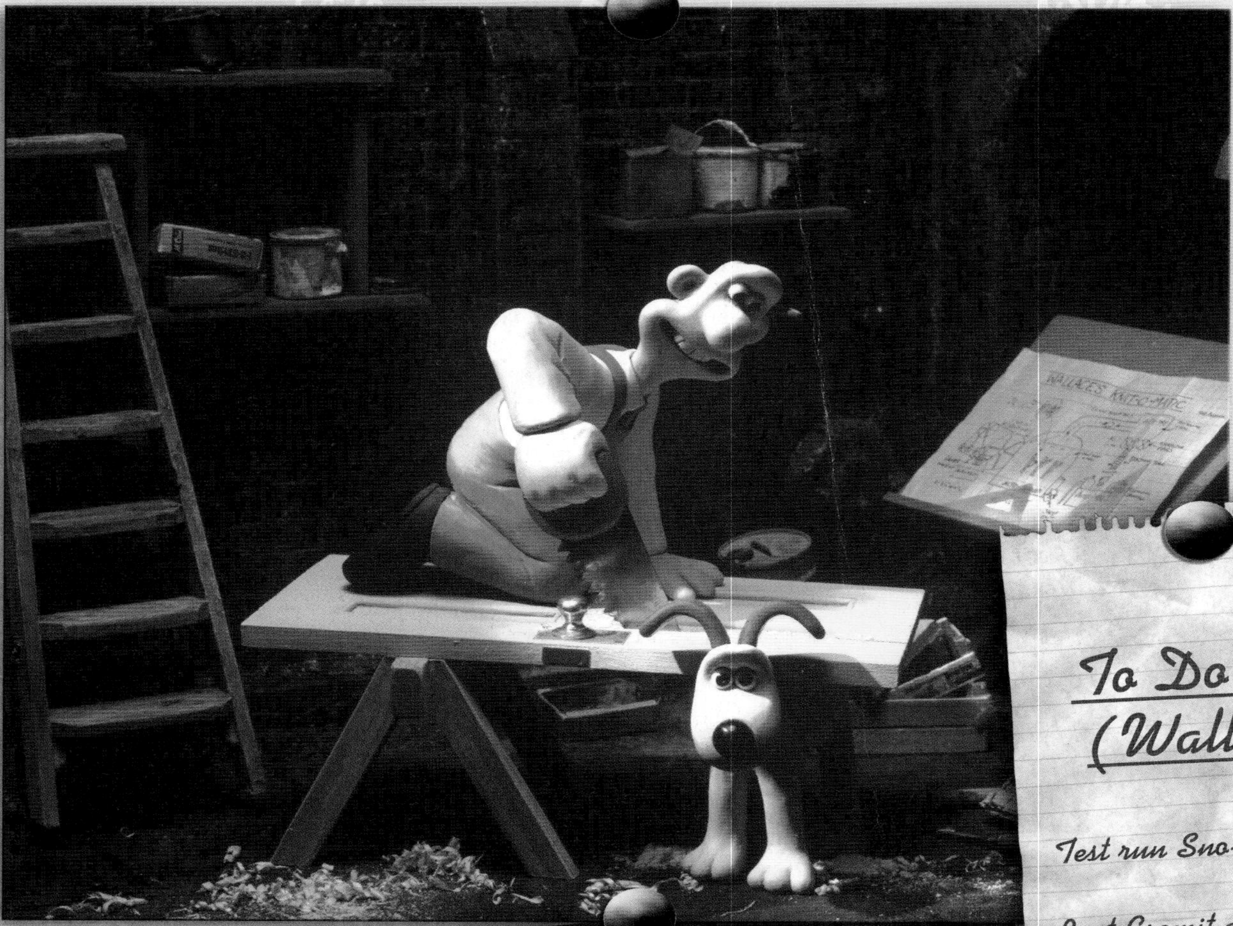

To Do List (Wallace)

Test run Sno-Blo Skis

Beat Gromit at 'Super Sleuth' (for once)

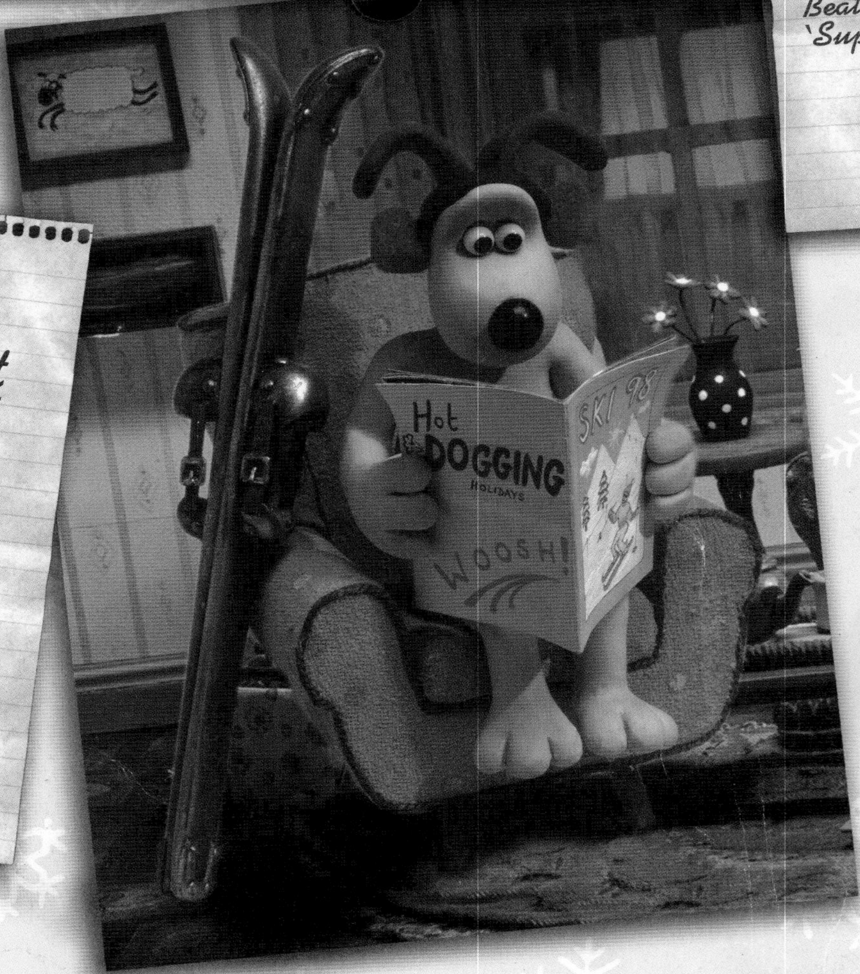
Hot DOGGING
HOLIDAYS
WOOSH!
SKI 98

To Do List (Gromit)

Plan winter break (not leg)

Beat Wallace at 'Super Sleuth' (as usual)

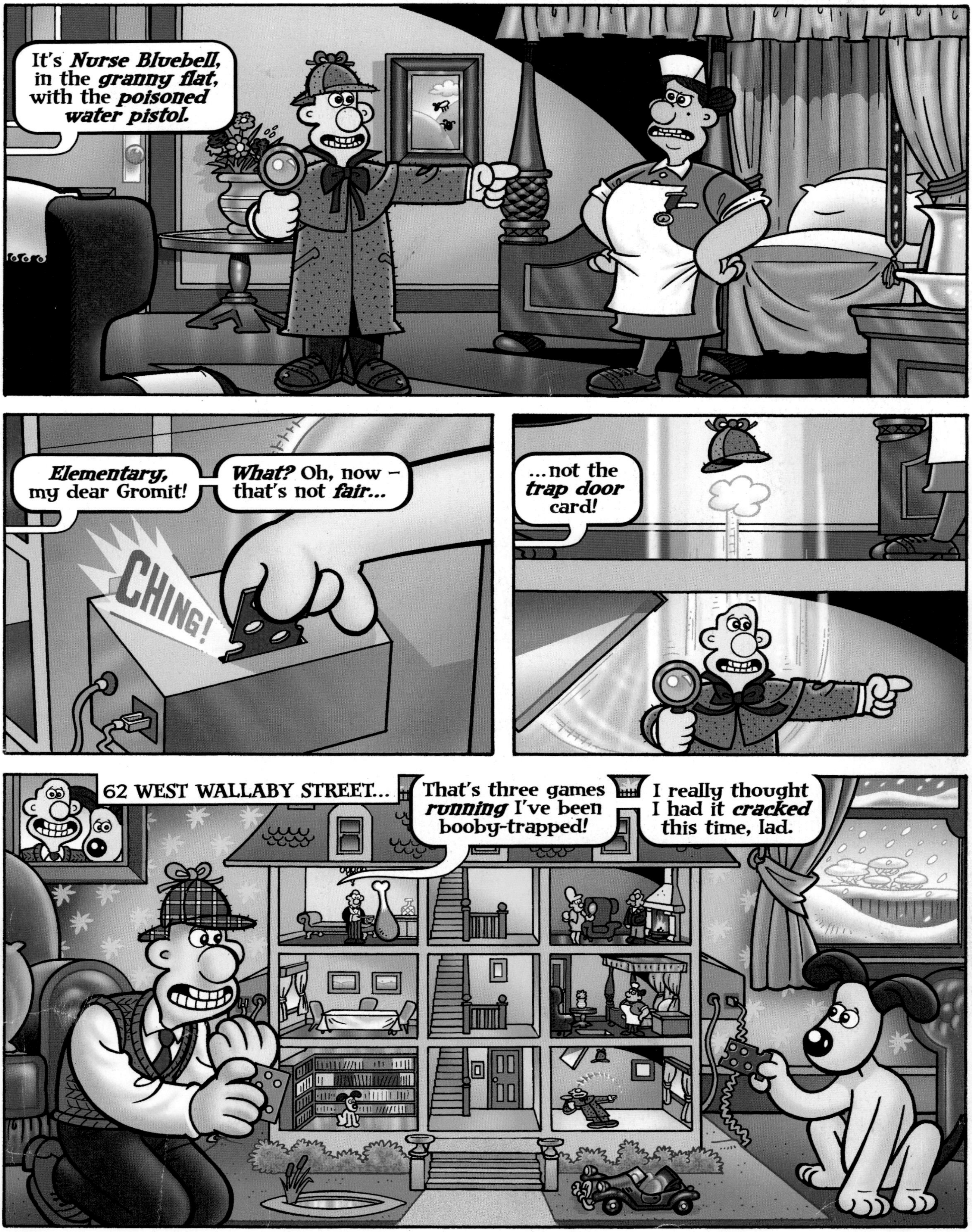
It's *Nurse Bluebell*, in the *granny flat*, with the *poisoned water pistol.*
Elementary, my dear Gromit!
What? Oh, now – that's not *fair...*
CHING!
...not the *trap door* card!
62 WEST WALLABY STREET...
That's three games *running* I've been booby-trapped!
I really thought I had it *cracked* this time, lad.

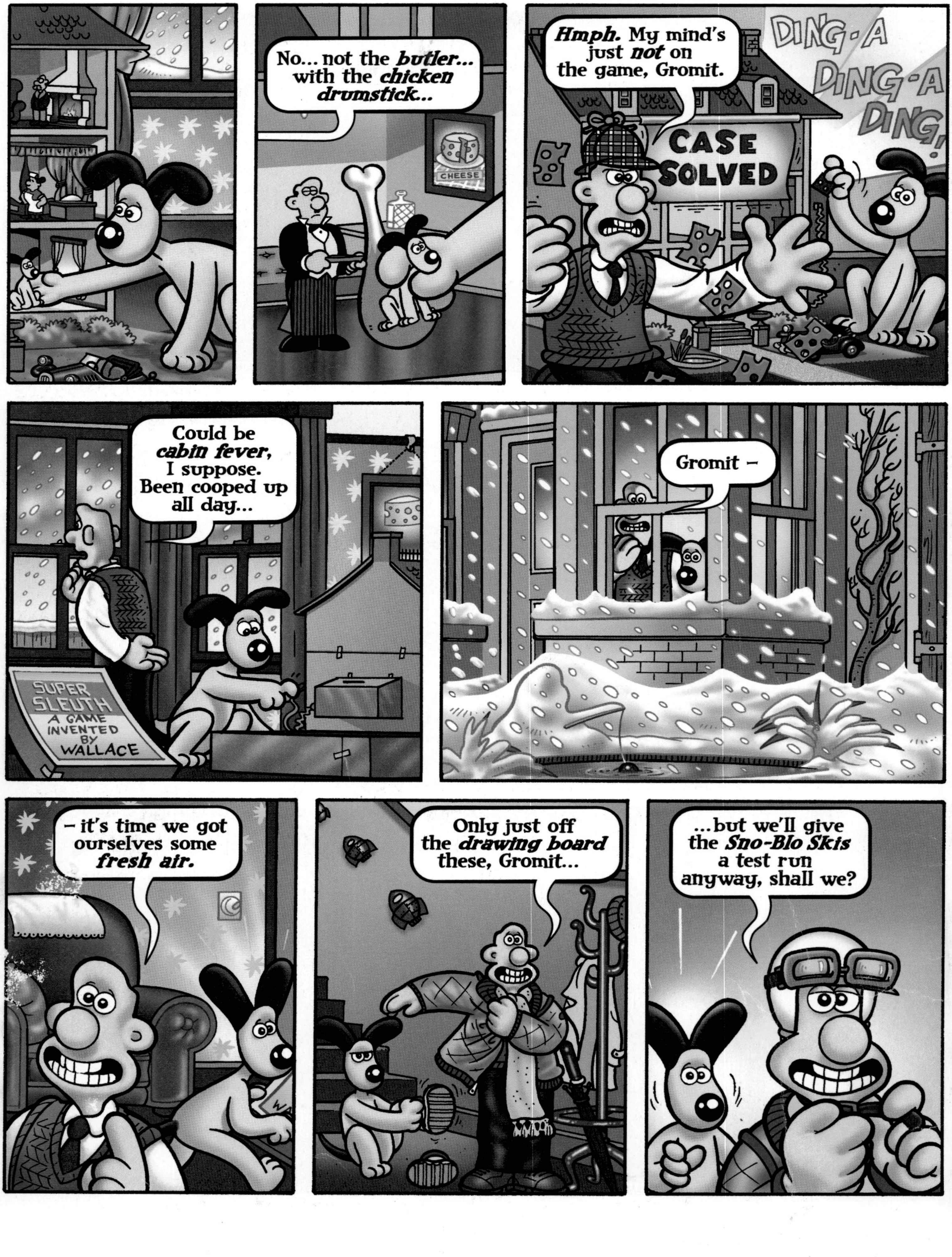

No... not the butler... with the chicken drumstick...
CHEESE
Hmph. My mind's just not on the game, Gromit.
CASE SOLVED
DING-A DING-A DING!
Could be cabin fever, I suppose. Been cooped up all day...
SUPER SLEUTH A GAME INVENTED BY WALLACE
Gromit –
– it's time we got ourselves some fresh air.
Only just off the drawing board these, Gromit...
...but we'll give the Sno-Blo Skis a test run anyway, shall we?

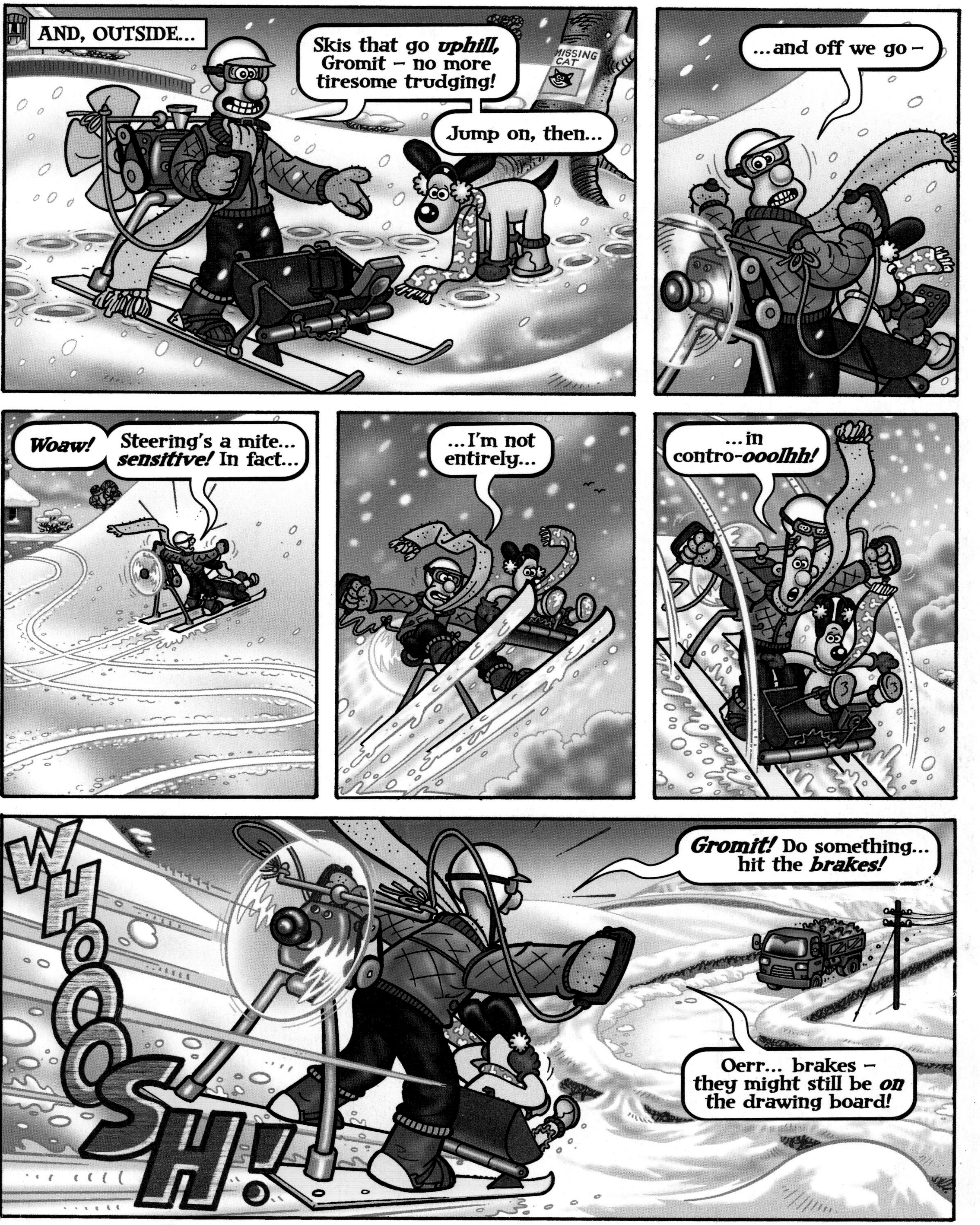
AND, OUTSIDE...
Skis that go *uphill*, Gromit – no more tiresome trudging!
MISSING CAT
Jump on, then...
...and off we go –
Woaw!
Steering's a mite... *sensitive!* In fact...
...I'm not entirely...
...in contro-*ooolhh!*
WHOOOSH!
Gromit! Do something... hit the *brakes!*
Oerr... brakes – they might still be *on* the drawing board!

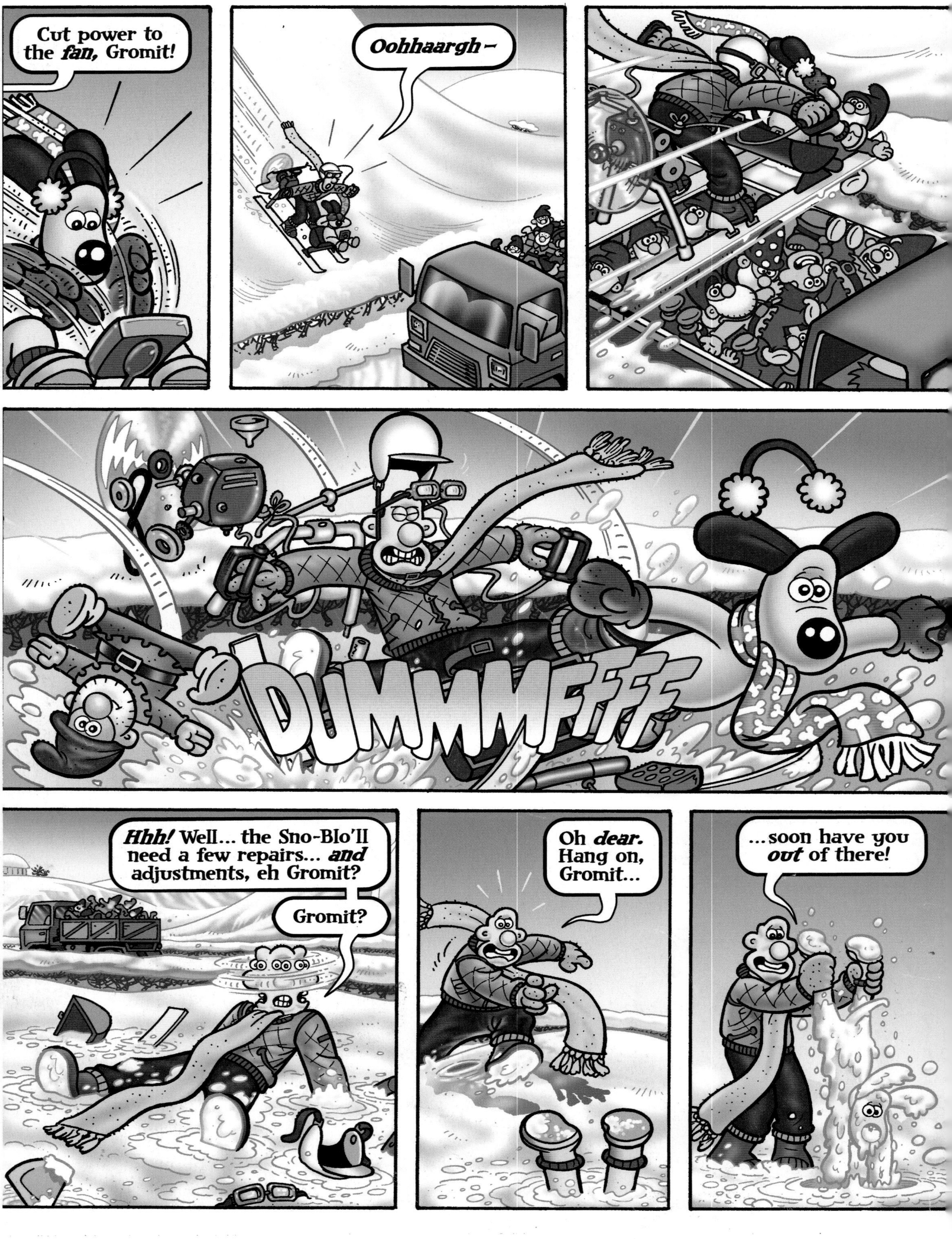

Cut power to the *fan*, Gromit!
Oohhaargh—
DUMMMFFF
Hhh! Well... the Sno-Blo'll need a few repairs... *and* adjustments, eh Gromit?
Gromit?
Oh *dear.* Hang on, Gromit...
...soon have you *out* of there!

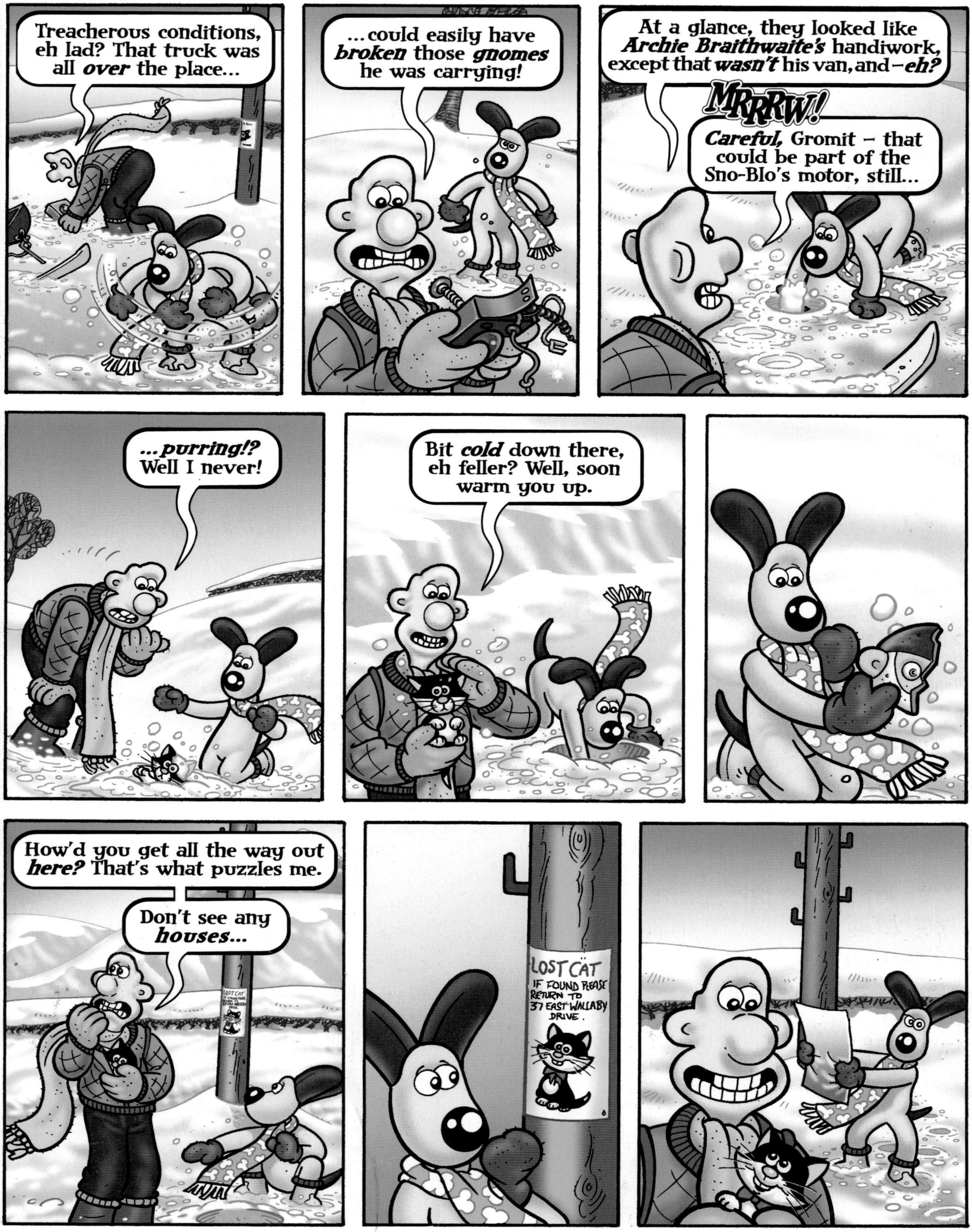

Treacherous conditions, eh lad? That truck was all *over* the place...
...could easily have *broken* those *gnomes* he was carrying!
At a glance, they looked like *Archie Braithwaite's* handiwork, except that *wasn't* his van, and – *eh?*
MRRRW!
Careful, Gromit – that could be part of the Sno-Blo's motor, still...
...purring!? Well I never!
Bit *cold* down there, eh feller? Well, soon warm you up.
How'd you get all the way out *here?* That's what puzzles me.
Don't see any *houses*...
LOST CAT
IF FOUND PLEASE RETURN TO 37 EAST WALLABY DRIVE.

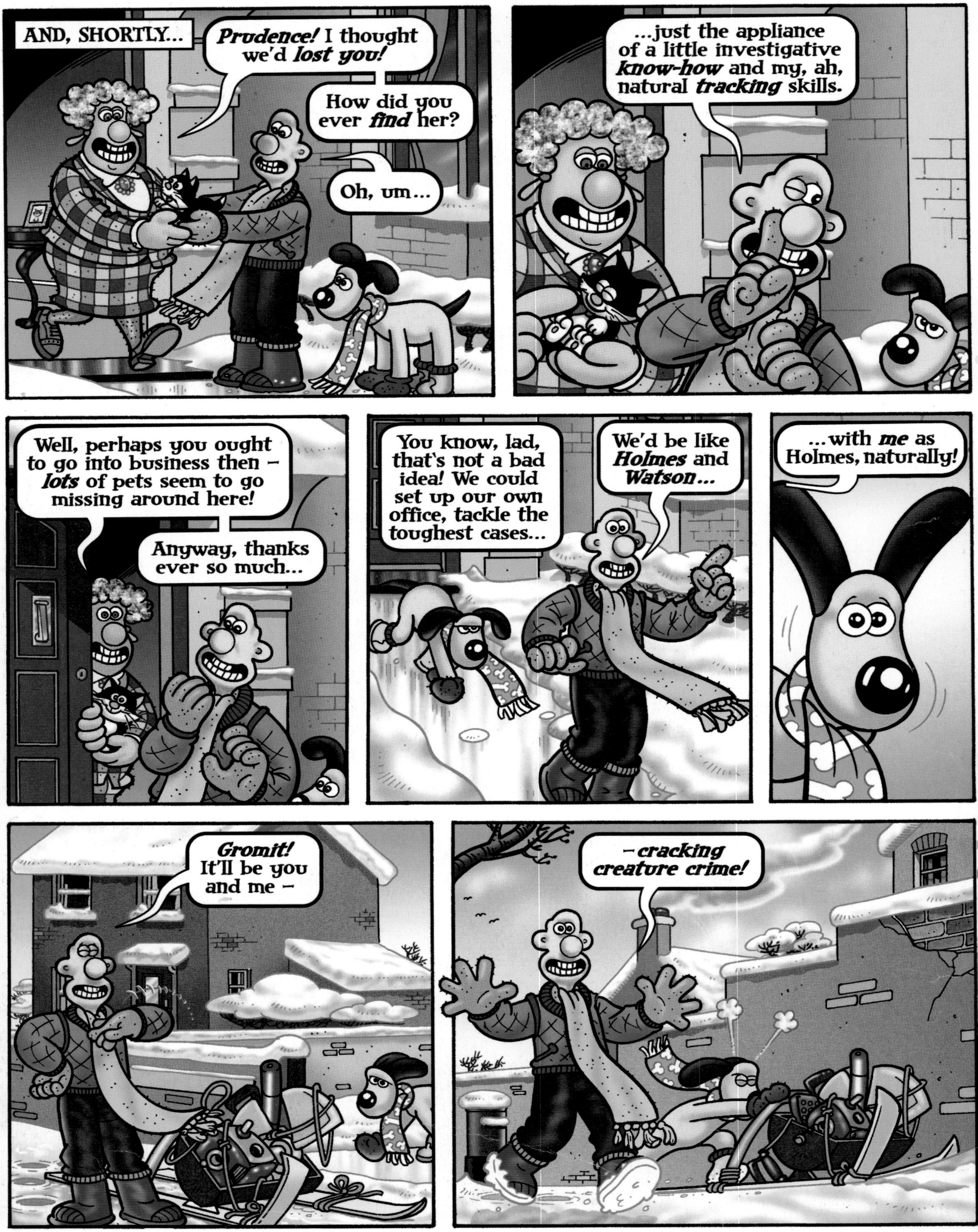

AND, SHORTLY...
Prudence! I thought we'd lost you!
How did you ever find her?
Oh, um...
...just the appliance of a little investigative know-how and my, ah, natural tracking skills.
Well, perhaps you ought to go into business then – lots of pets seem to go missing around here!
Anyway, thanks ever so much...
You know, lad, that's not a bad idea! We could set up our own office, tackle the toughest cases...
We'd be like Holmes and Watson...
...with me as Holmes, naturally!
Gromit! It'll be you and me –
– cracking creature crime!

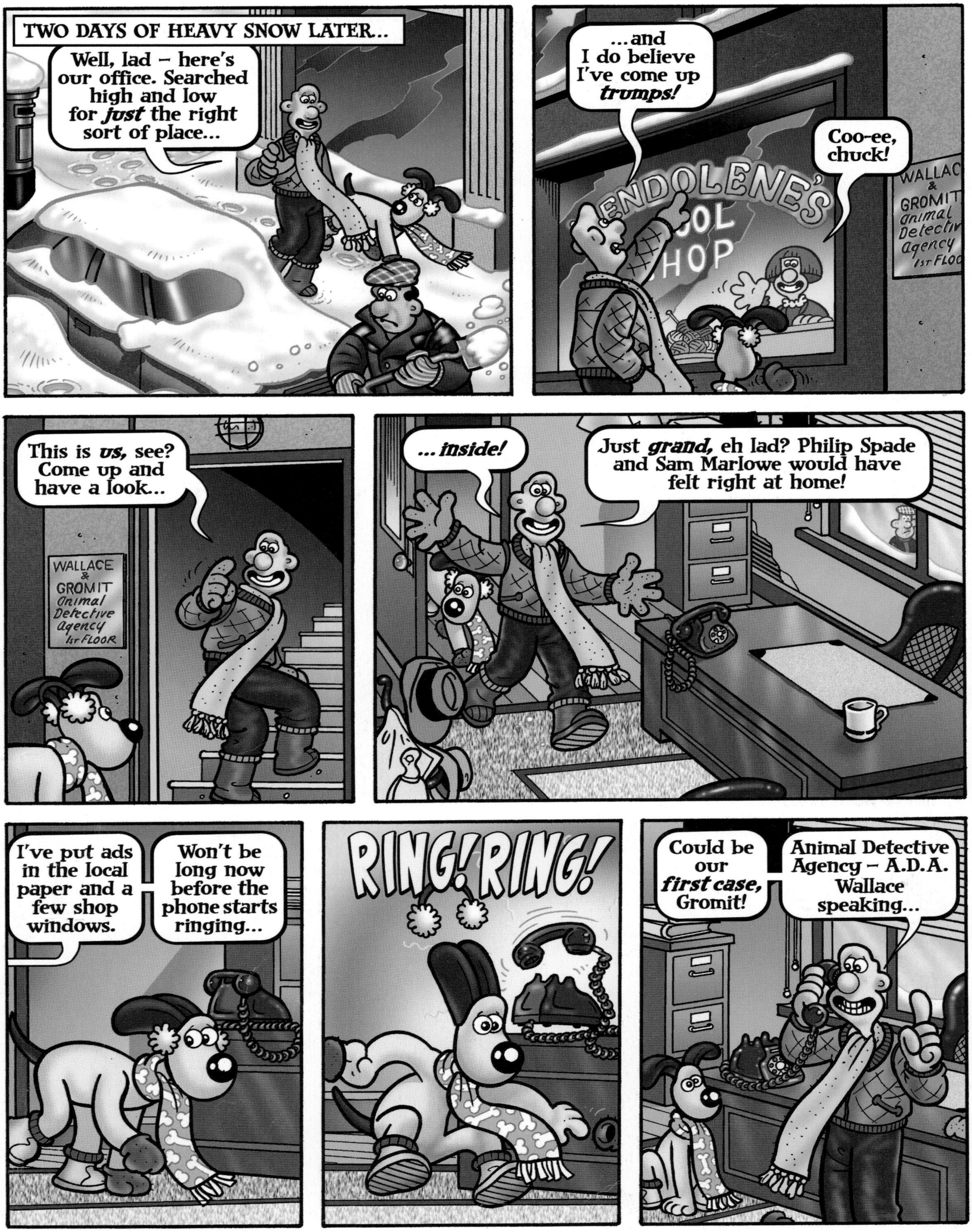

TWO DAYS OF HEAVY SNOW LATER...
Well, lad – here's our office. Searched high and low for *just* the right sort of place...
...and I do believe I've come up *trumps!*
Coo-ee, chuck!
ENDOLENE'S
OOL
HOP
WALLAC
&
GROMIT
Animal
Detectiv
agency
1ST FLOO
This is *us,* see? Come up and have a look...
WALLACE
&
GROMIT
Animal
Detective
agency
1ST FLOOR
...*inside!*
Just *grand,* eh lad? Philip Spade and Sam Marlowe would have felt right at home!
I've put ads in the local paper and a few shop windows.
Won't be long now before the phone starts ringing...
RING! RING!
Could be our *first case,* Gromit!
Animal Detective Agency – A.D.A. Wallace speaking...

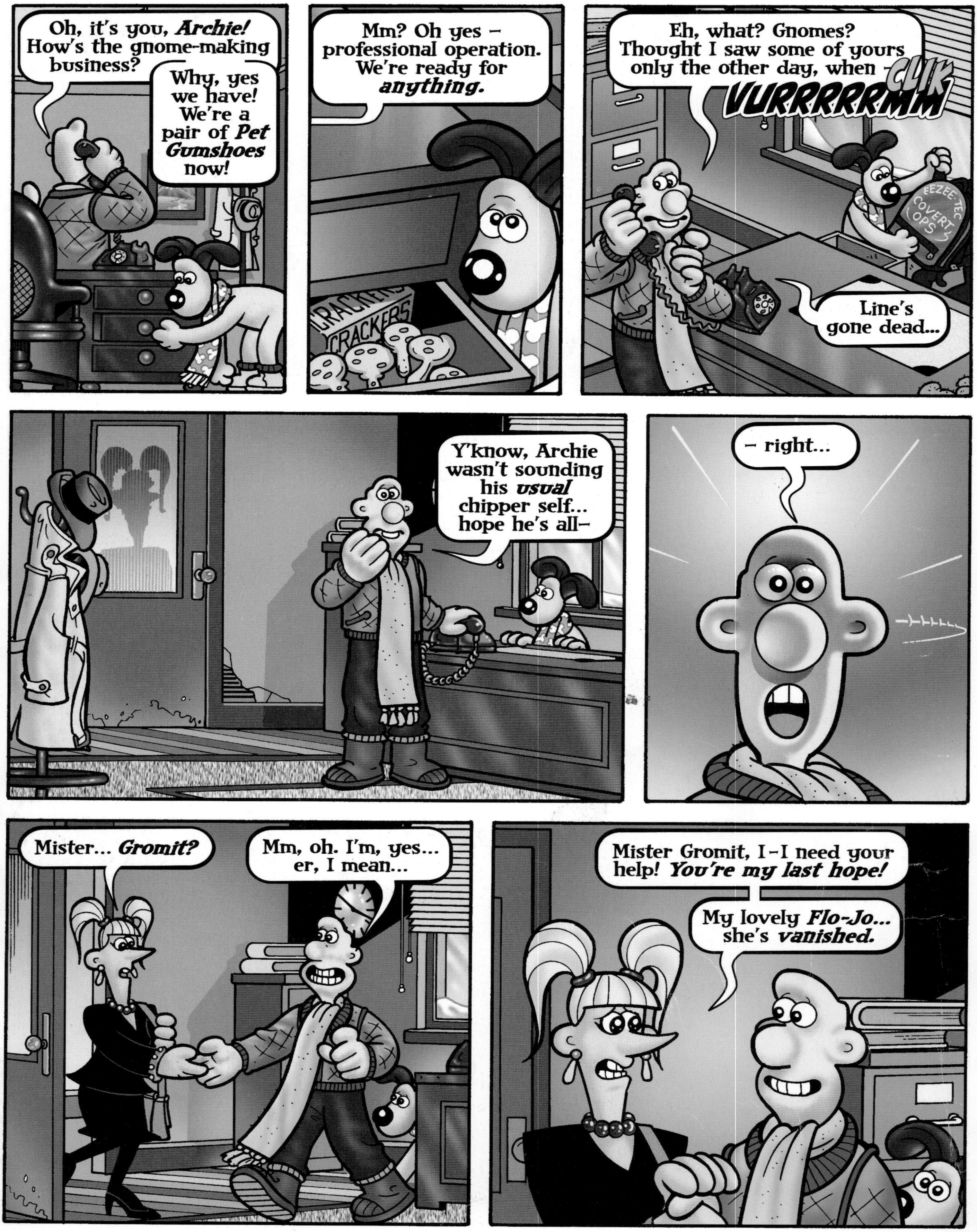

Oh, it's you, Archie! How's the gnome-making business?
Why, yes we have! We're a pair of Pet Gumshoes now!
Mm? Oh yes – professional operation. We're ready for anything.
Eh, what? Gnomes? Thought I saw some of yours only the other day, when –
CLIK
VURRRRRMM
EEZEE-TEC COVERT OPS
Line's gone dead...
Y'know, Archie wasn't sounding his usual chipper self... hope he's all–
– right...
Mister... Gromit?
Mm, oh. I'm, yes... er, I mean...
Mister Gromit, I–I need your help! You're my last hope!
My lovely Flo-Jo... she's vanished.

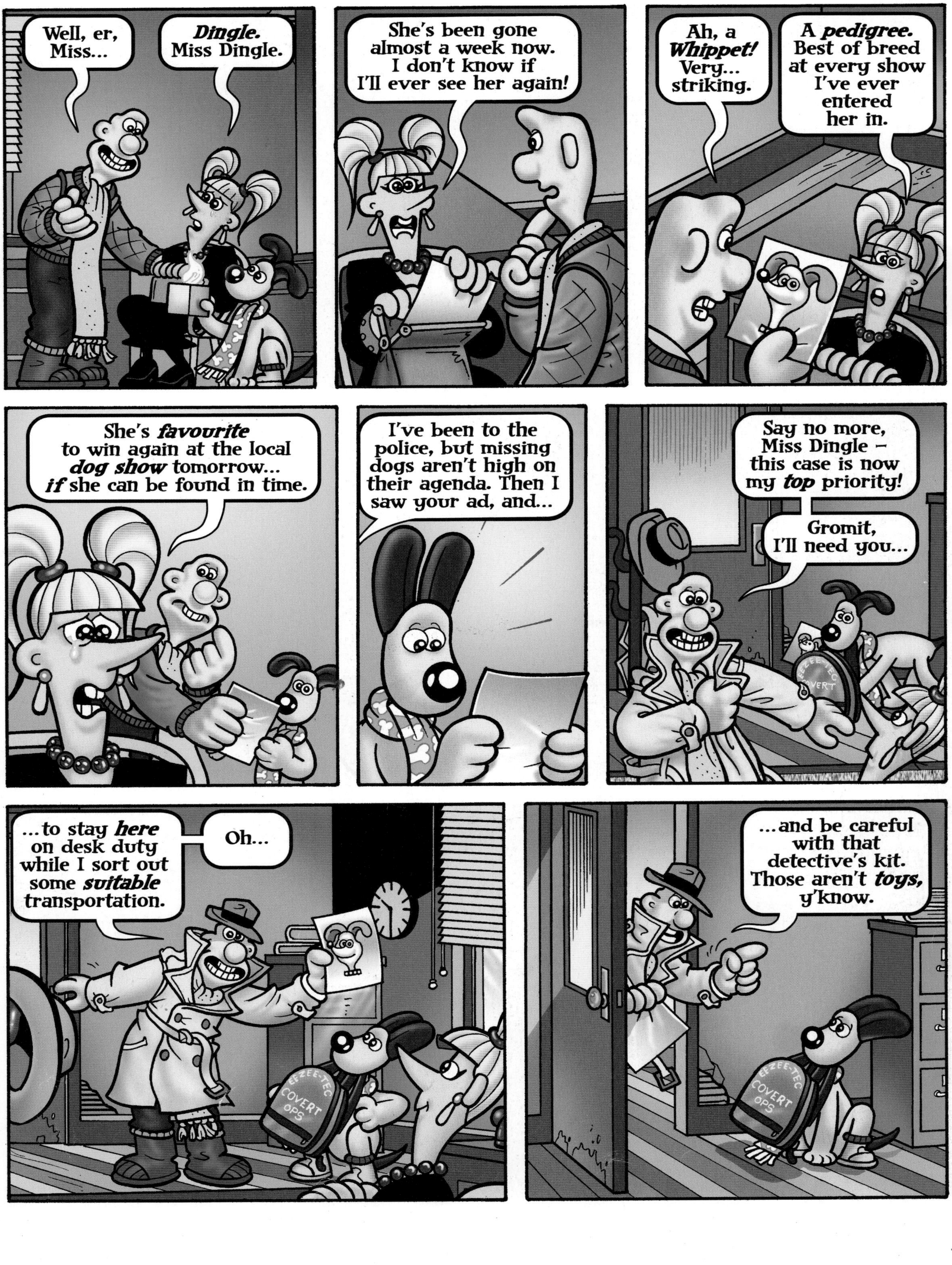
Well, er, Miss...
Dingle. Miss Dingle.
She's been gone almost a week now. I don't know if I'll ever see her again!
Ah, a *Whippet!* Very... striking.
A *pedigree.* Best of breed at every show I've ever entered her in.
She's *favourite* to win again at the local *dog show* tomorrow... *if* she can be found in time.
I've been to the police, but missing dogs aren't high on their agenda. Then I saw your ad, and...
Say no more, Miss Dingle – this case is now my *top* priority!
Gromit, I'll need you...
...to stay *here* on desk duty while I sort out some *suitable* transportation.
Oh...
...and be careful with that detective's kit. Those aren't *toys,* y'know.
EEZEE-TEC COVERT OPS

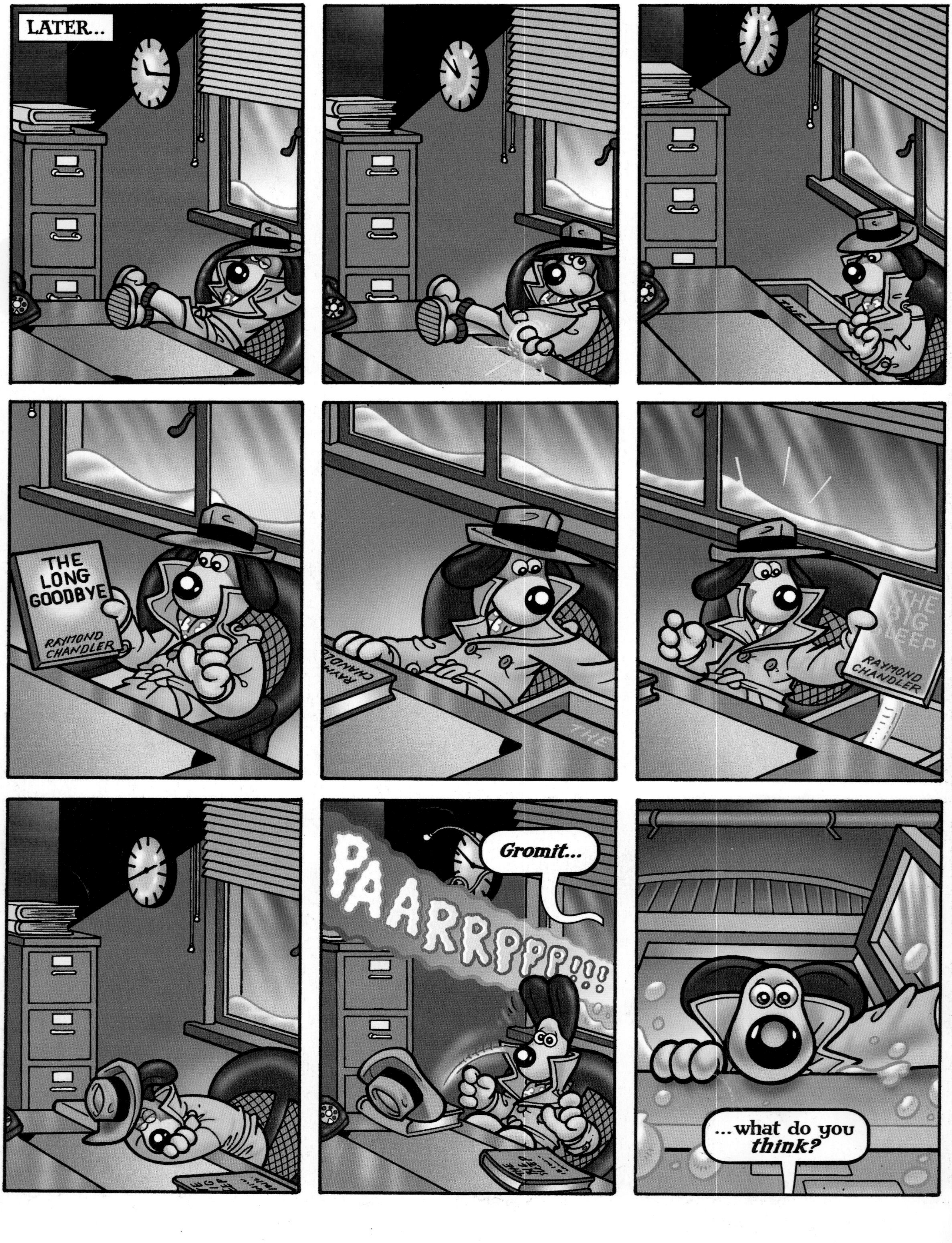
LATER...
THE LONG GOODBYE
RAYMOND CHANDLER
THE BIG SLEEP
RAYMOND CHANDLER
PAARRPPP!!!
Gromit...
...what do you think?

My *Winter Warmer Snow Plough*! Guaranteed to keep you *moving*, whatever the conditions!

So, without further ado, I'm off to *interview* potential witnesses. Can't let the case go *cold*, can we?

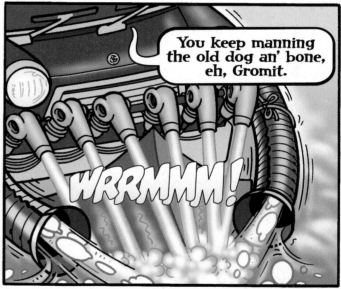

You keep manning the old dog an' bone, eh, Gromit.

WRRMMM!

FRESH BREAD

THWFFF

SLAM!

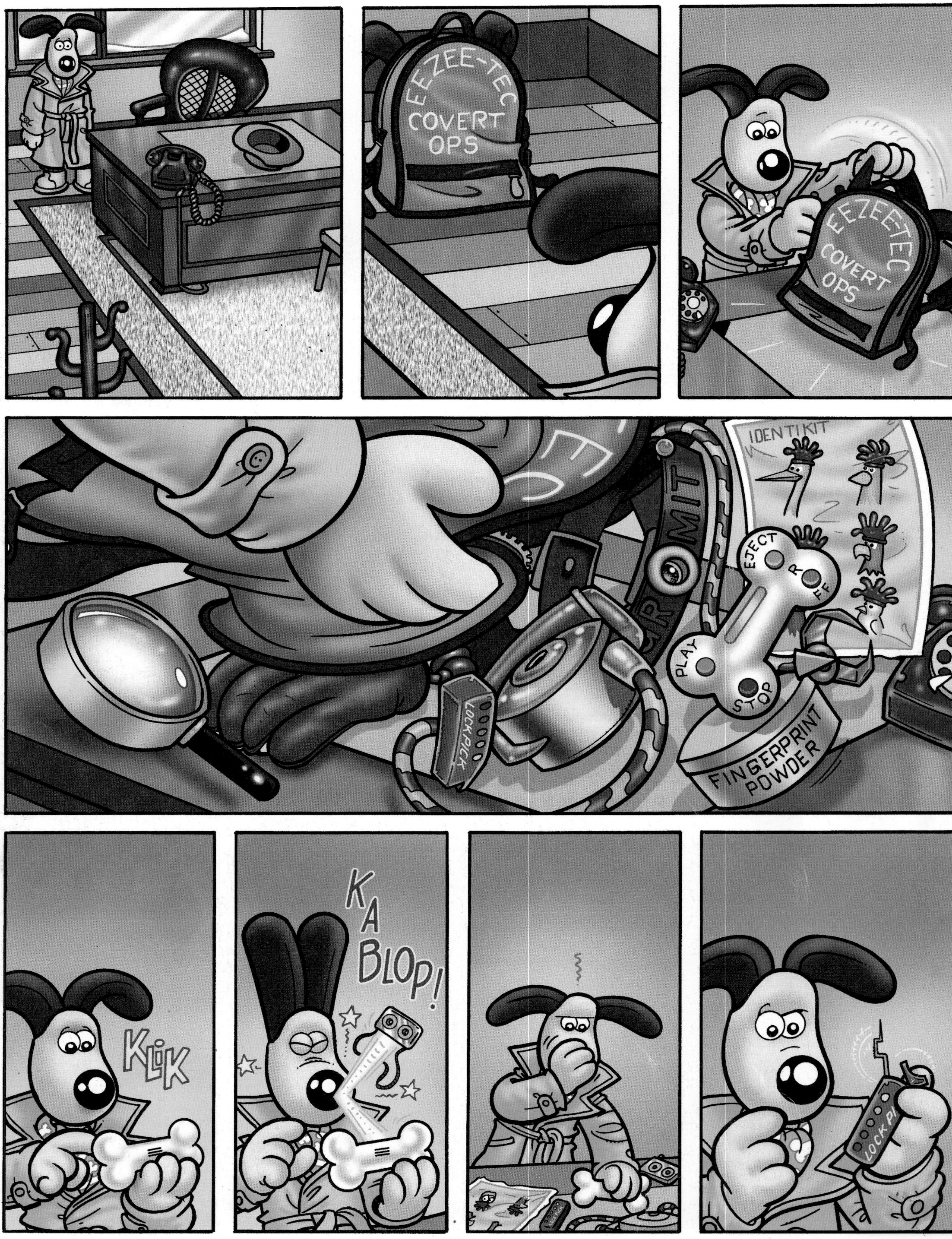
EEZEE-TEC
COVERT
OPS
EEZEE-TEC
COVERT
OPS
IDENTIKIT
EJECT
PLAY
STOP
LOCK PICK
FINGERPRINT
POWDER
KLIK
KA
BLOP!

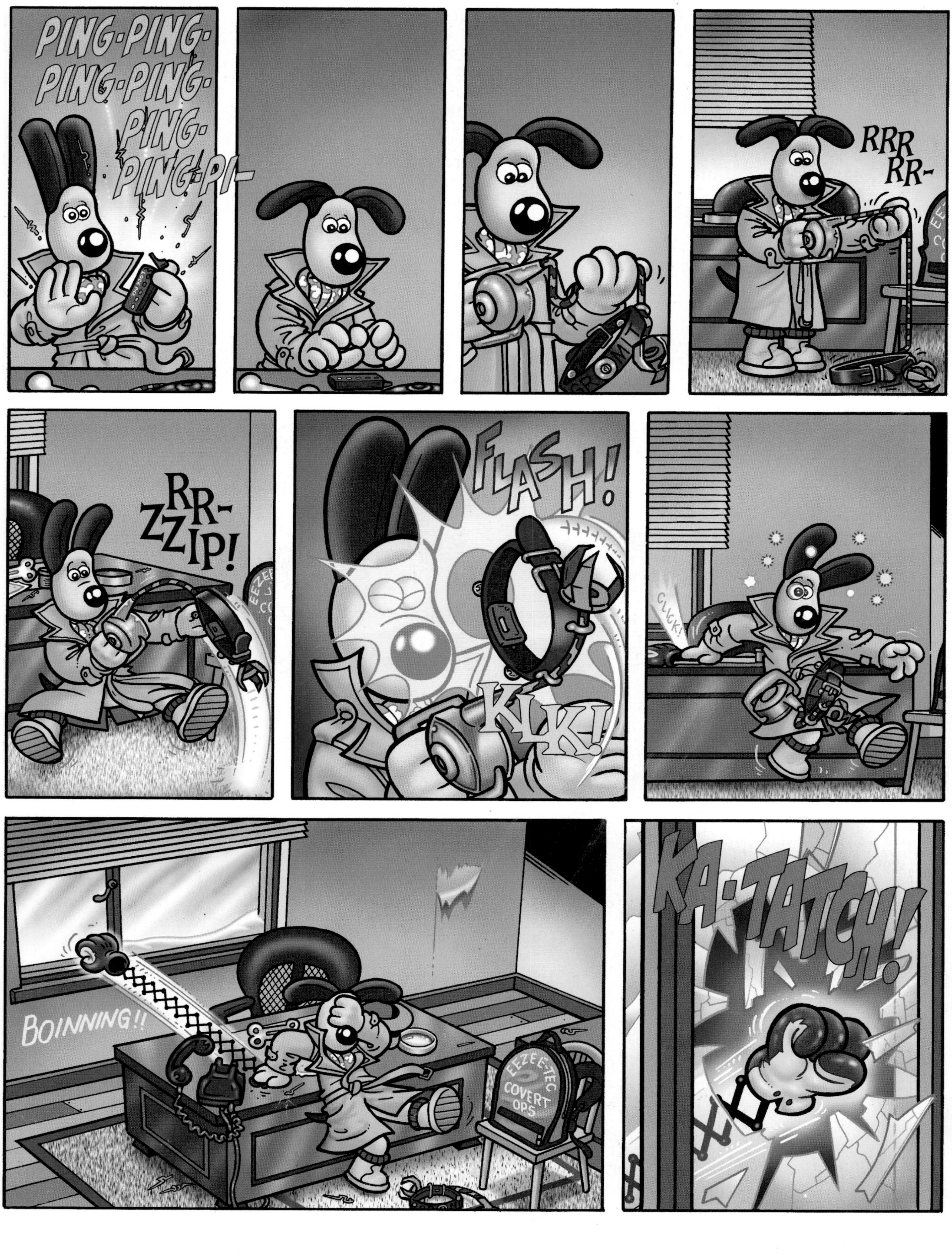
PING-PING-
PING-PING-
PING-
PING-PI-
RRR
RR-
RR-
ZZIP!
FLASH!
KLIK!
CLICK!
BOINNING!!
EEZEE-TEC
COVERT
OPS
KA-TATCH!

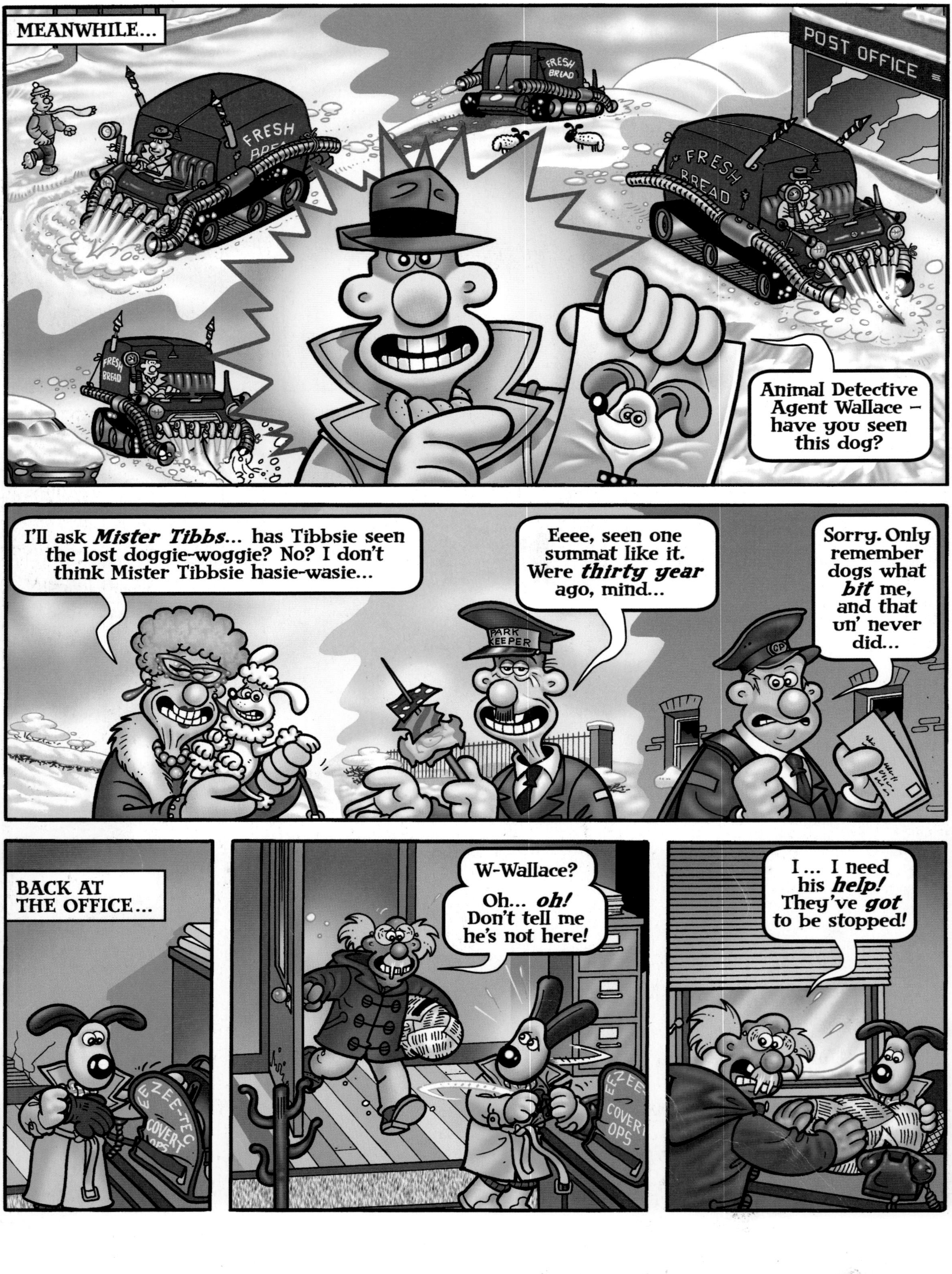
MEANWHILE...
POST OFFICE
FRESH BREAD
FRESH BREAD
FRESH BREAD
FRESH BREAD
Animal Detective Agent Wallace – have you seen this dog?
I'll ask *Mister Tibbs*... has Tibbsie seen the lost doggie-woggie? No? I don't think Mister Tibbsie hasie-wasie...
PARK KEEPER
Eeee, seen one summat like it. Were *thirty year* ago, mind...
Sorry. Only remember dogs what *bit* me, and that un' never did...
BACK AT THE OFFICE...
EEZEE-TEC COVERT OPS
W-Wallace?
Oh... *oh!* Don't tell me he's not here!
EEZEE COVERT OPS
I... I need his *help!* They've *got* to be stopped!

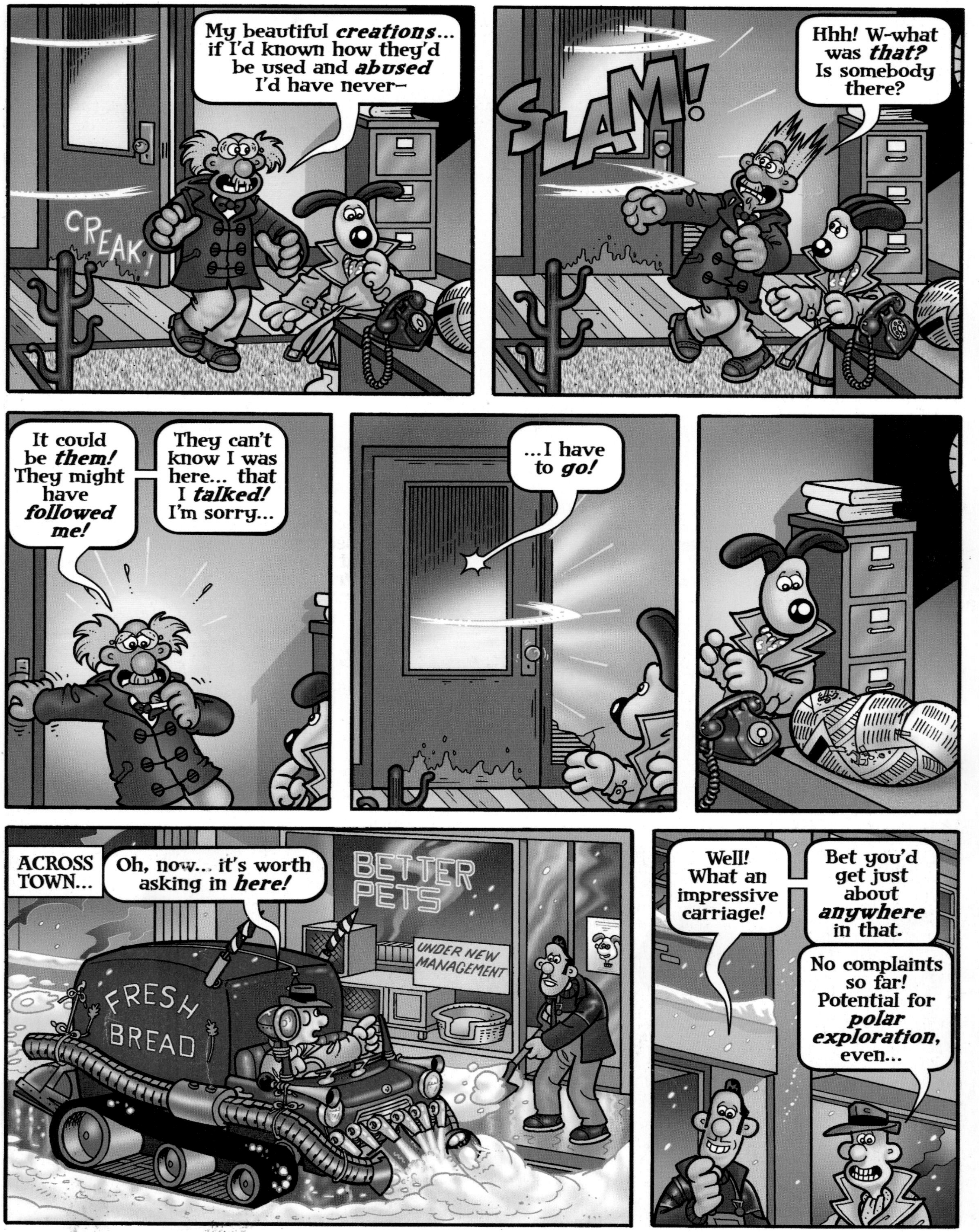
My beautiful *creations*... if I'd known how they'd be used and *abused* I'd have never–
CREAK!
SLAM!
Hhh! W-what was *that?* Is somebody there?
It could be *them!* They might have *followed* me!
They can't know I was here... that I *talked!* I'm sorry...
...I have to *go!*
ACROSS TOWN...
Oh, now... it's worth asking in *here!*
BETTER PETS
UNDER NEW MANAGEMENT
FRESH BREAD
Well! What an impressive carriage!
Bet you'd get just about *anywhere* in that.
No complaints so far! Potential for *polar exploration*, even...

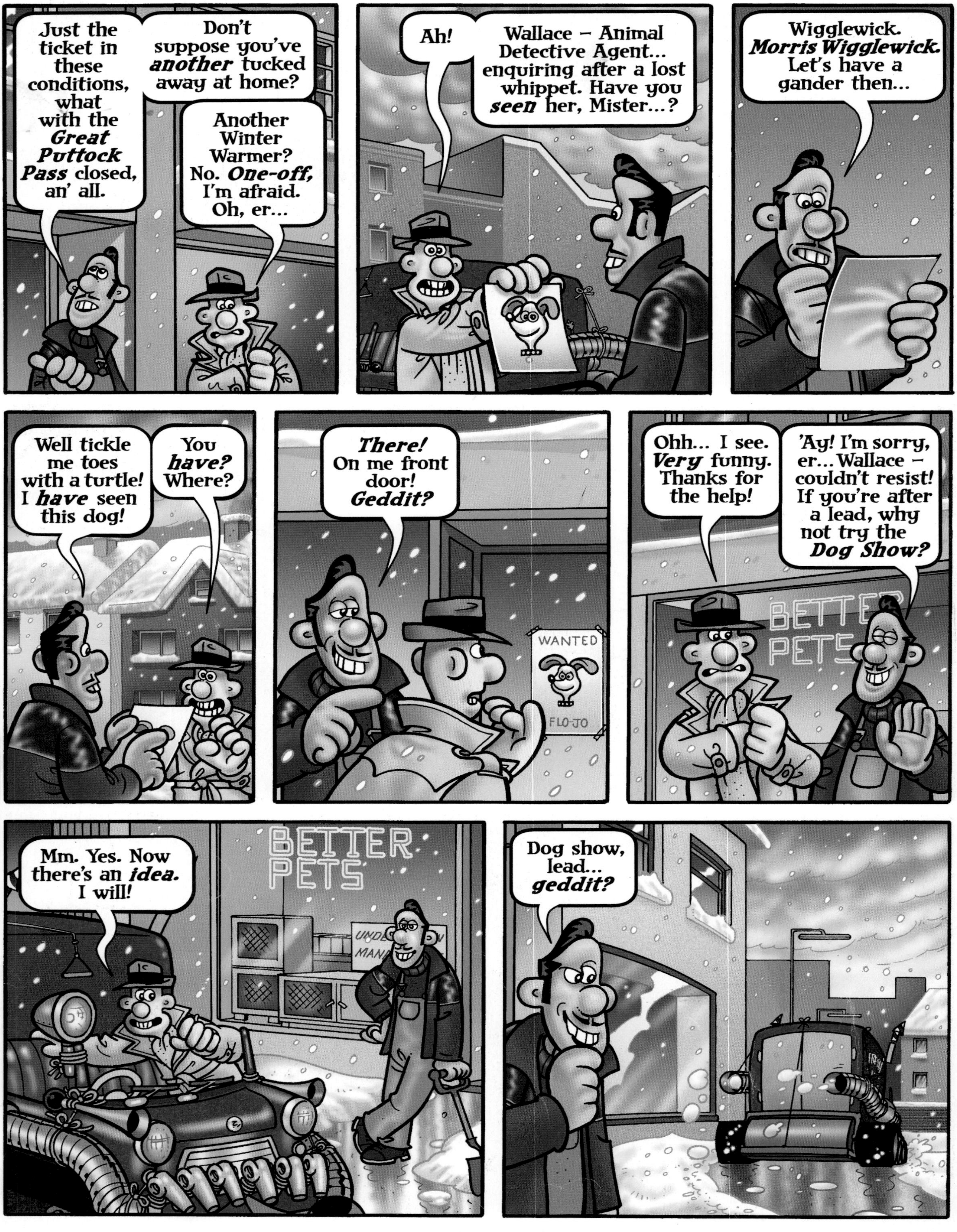
Just the ticket in these conditions, what with the Great Puttock Pass closed, an' all.
Don't suppose you've another tucked away at home?
Another Winter Warmer? No. One-off, I'm afraid. Oh, er...
Ah!
Wallace – Animal Detective Agent... enquiring after a lost whippet. Have you seen her, Mister...?
Wigglewick. Morris Wigglewick. Let's have a gander then...
Well tickle me toes with a turtle! I have seen this dog!
You have? Where?
There! On me front door! Geddit?
WANTED
FLO-JO
Ohh... I see. Very funny. Thanks for the help!
'Ay! I'm sorry, er... Wallace – couldn't resist! If you're after a lead, why not try the Dog Show?
BETTER PETS
Mm. Yes. Now there's an idea. I will!
BETTER PETS
Dog show, lead... geddit?

MEANWHILE...

CLICK!

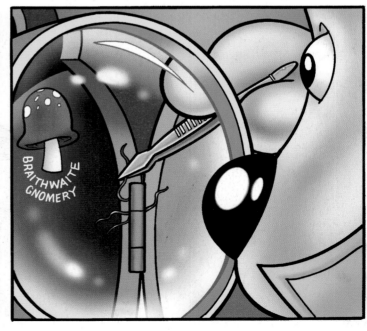

BRAITHWAITE GNOMERY

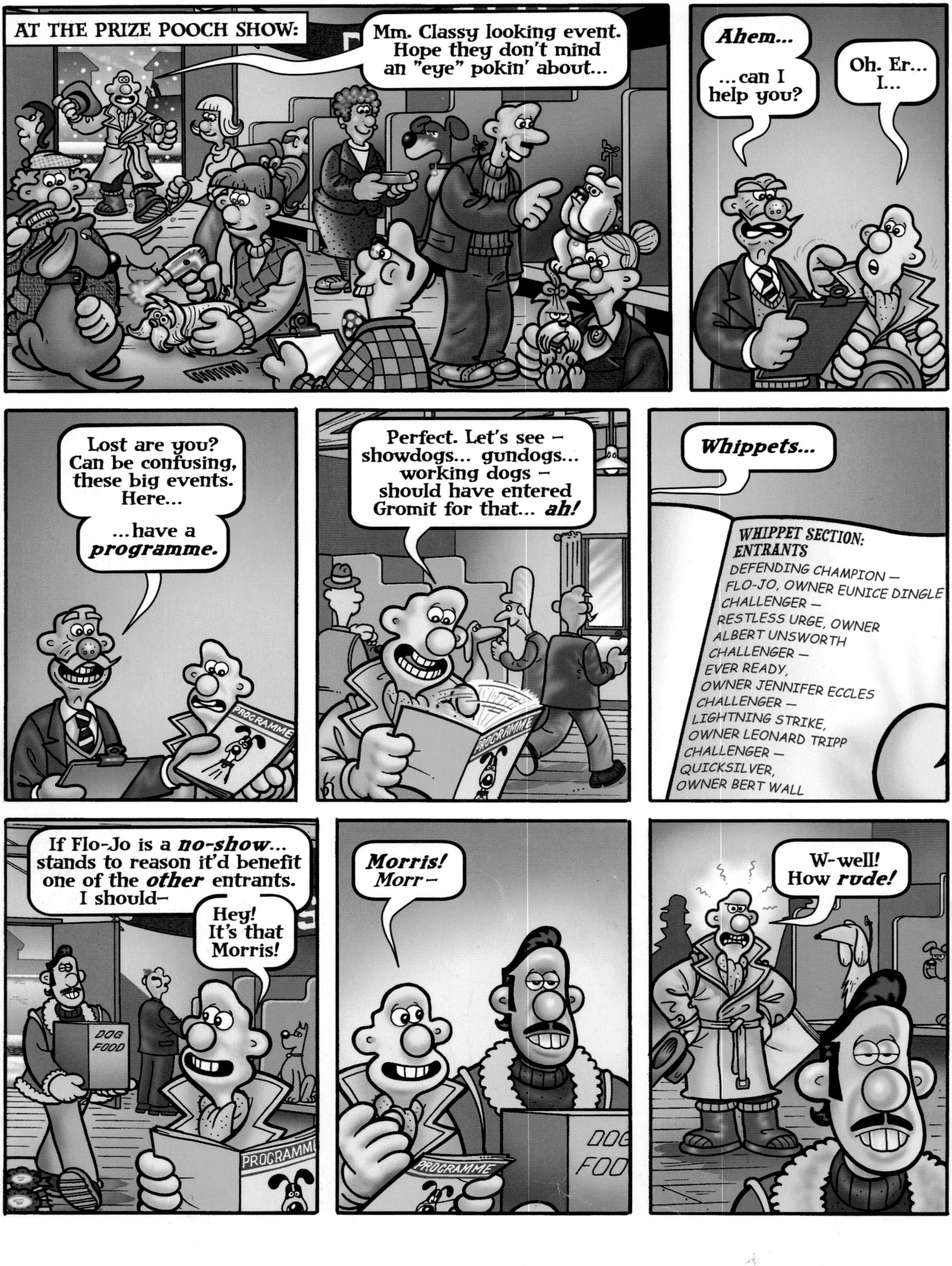
AT THE PRIZE POOCH SHOW:
Mm. Classy looking event. Hope they don't mind an "eye" pokin' about...
Ahem...
...can I help you?
Oh. Er... I...
Lost are you? Can be confusing, these big events. Here...
...have a programme.
PROGRAMME
Perfect. Let's see – showdogs... gundogs... working dogs – should have entered Gromit for that... ah!
PROGRAMME
Whippets...
WHIPPET SECTION: ENTRANTS
DEFENDING CHAMPION – FLO-JO, OWNER EUNICE DINGLE
CHALLENGER – RESTLESS URGE, OWNER ALBERT UNSWORTH
CHALLENGER – EVER READY, OWNER JENNIFER ECCLES
CHALLENGER – LIGHTNING STRIKE, OWNER LEONARD TRIPP
CHALLENGER – QUICKSILVER, OWNER BERT WALL
If Flo-Jo is a no-show... stands to reason it'd benefit one of the other entrants. I should–
Hey! It's that Morris!
DOG FOOD
PROGRAMME
Morris! Morr–
PROGRAMME
W-well! How rude!

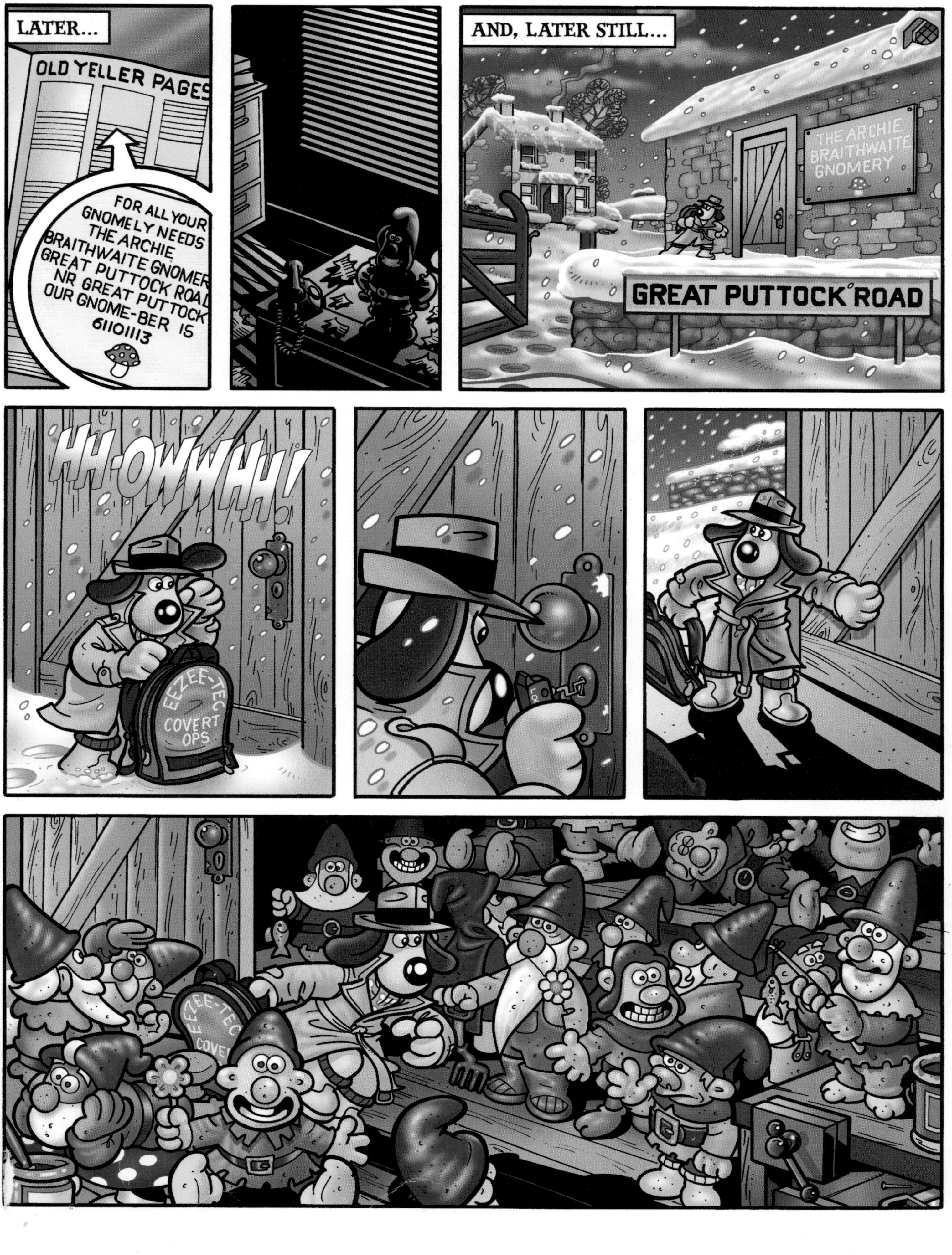
LATER...
OLD YELLER PAGES
FOR ALL YOUR GNOMELY NEEDS THE ARCHIE BRAITHWAITE GNOMER GREAT PUTTOCK ROAD NR GREAT PUTTOCK OUR GNOME-BER IS 6110113
AND, LATER STILL...
THE ARCHIE BRAITHWAITE GNOMERY
GREAT PUTTOCK ROAD
HH-OWWHH!
EEZEE-TEC COVERT OPS
EEZEE-TEC COVER

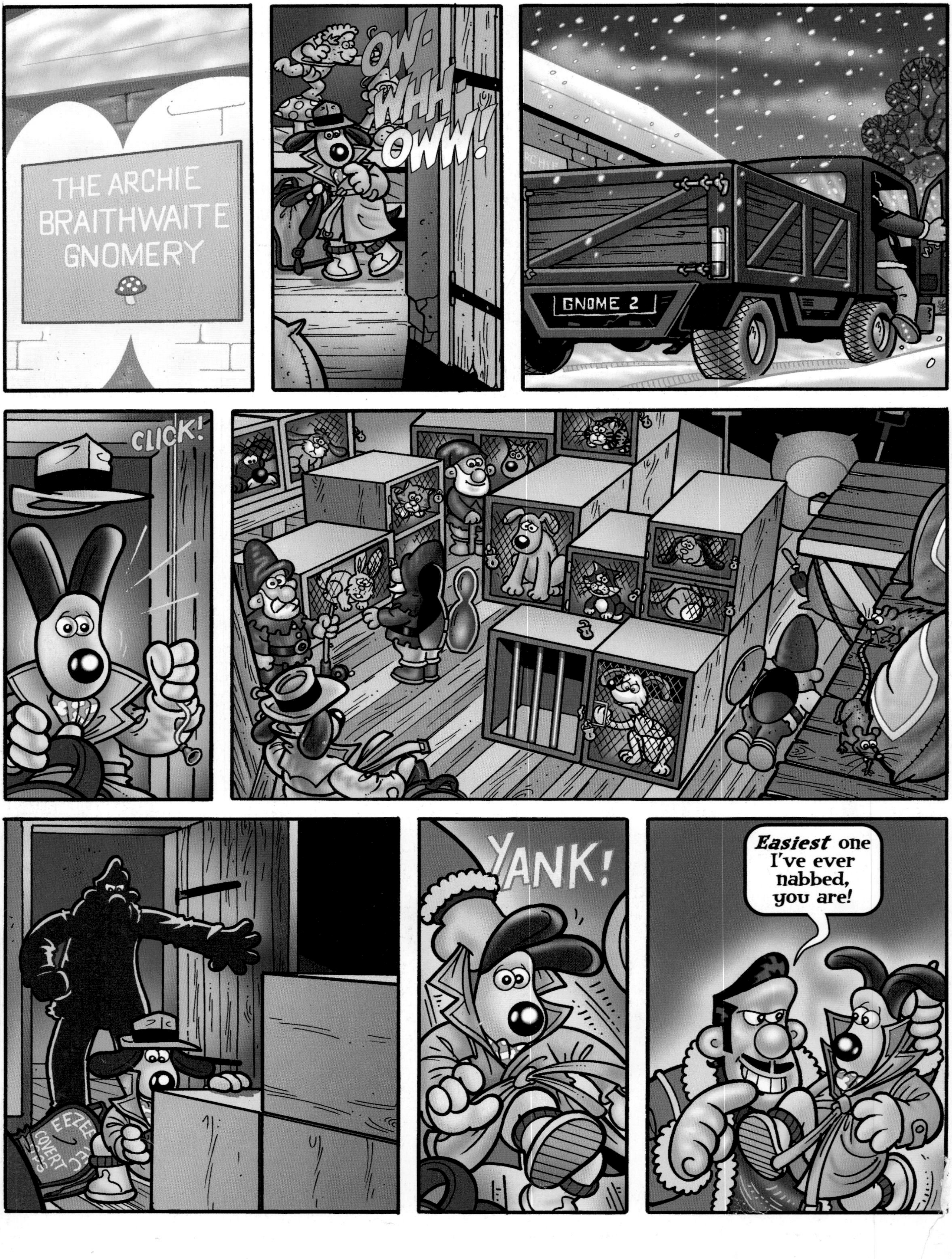
THE ARCHIE BRAITHWAITE GNOMERY
OW-WHH-OWW!
ARCHIE
GNOME 2
CLICK!
EEZEE COVERT
YANK!
Easiest one I've ever nabbed, you are!

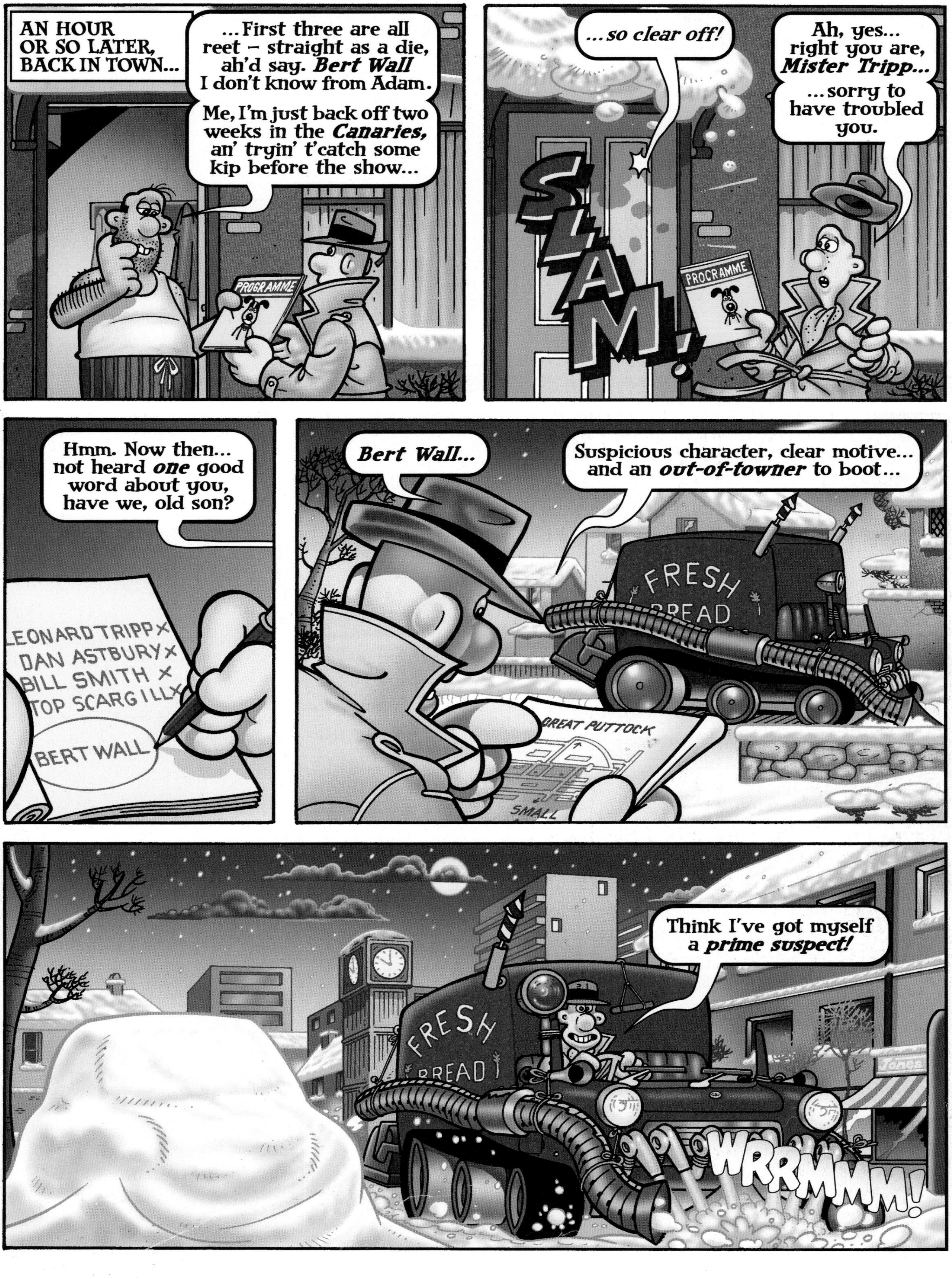
AN HOUR OR SO LATER, BACK IN TOWN...
...First three are all reet – straight as a die, ah'd say. Bert Wall I don't know from Adam.
Me, I'm just back off two weeks in the Canaries, an' tryin' t'catch some kip before the show...
PROGRAMME
...so clear off!
SLAM!
PROGRAMME
Ah, yes... right you are, Mister Tripp...
...sorry to have troubled you.
Hmm. Now then... not heard one good word about you, have we, old son?
LEONARD TRIPP X
DAN ASTBURY X
BILL SMITH X
TOP SCARGILL X
BERT WALL
Bert Wall...
Suspicious character, clear motive... and an out-of-towner to boot...
FRESH BREAD
GREAT PUTTOCK
SMALL
Think I've got myself a prime suspect!
FRESH BREAD
WRRMMMM!

SHORTLY...

That'll be the phone. Could be Miss Dingle, after a progress report.

RING RING RING RING RING!

WENDOLENE'S WOOL SHOP

Why isn't Gromit picking *up?*

RING-RING-RING-RING-

What's the point in having a loyal aide...

...if he's not aiding!

PLANET

hnh-hnh- RING-RING-RI-

Oh... *blast!*

Gromit? Where are you, lad? And what's one of Archie's *gnomes* doing sat here?

Hmm. Only one way to find out...

Hello, Archie – it's Wallace. Sorry to call you so *late.* I just wondered, have you seen Gromit?

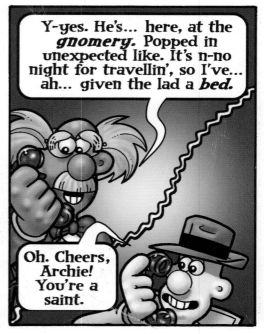

Y-yes. He's... here, at the *gnomery.* Popped in unexpected like. It's n-no night for travellin', so I've... ah... given the lad a *bed.*

Oh. Cheers, Archie! You're a saint.

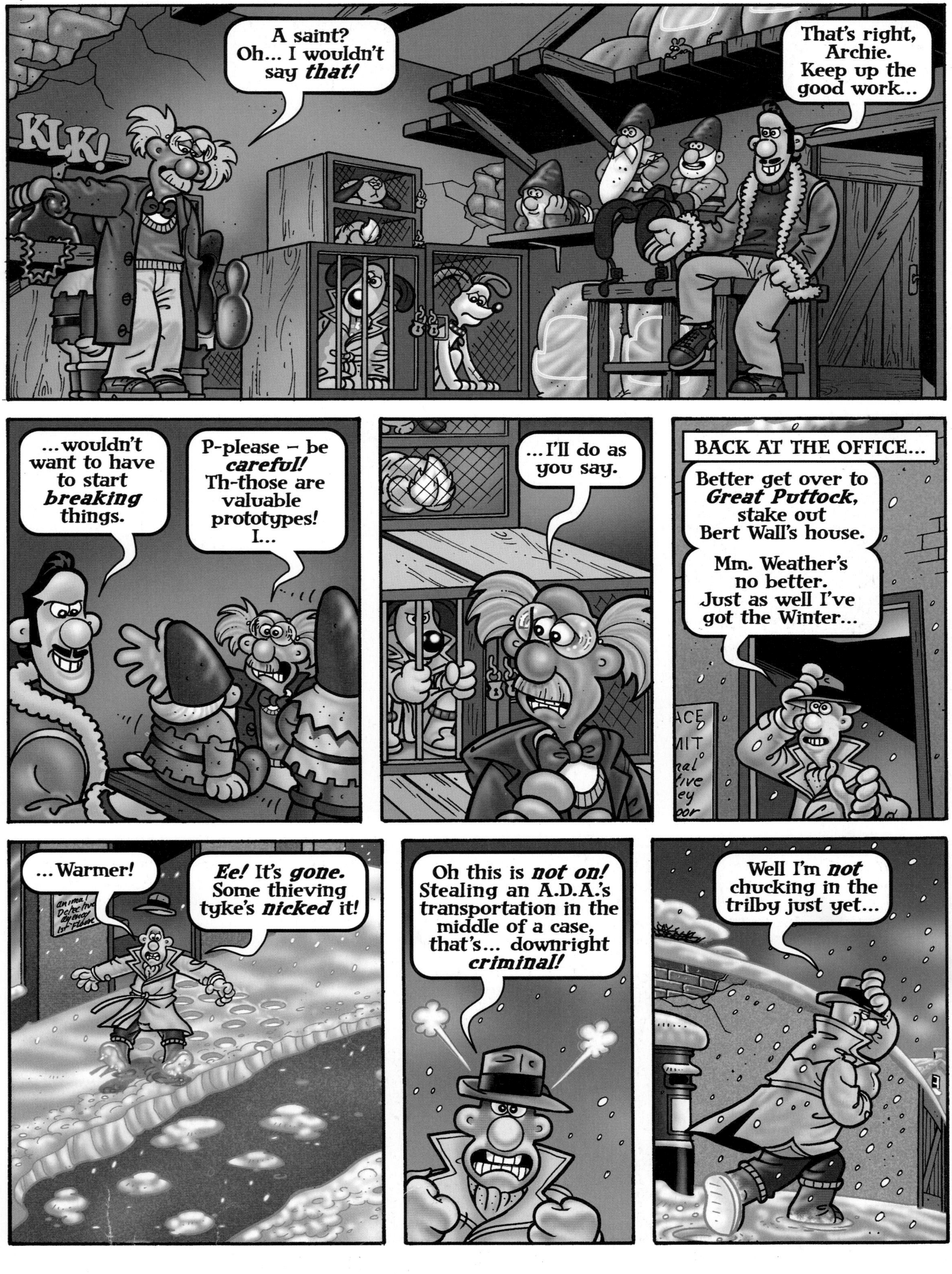
KLK!
A saint? Oh... I wouldn't say *that!*
That's right, Archie. Keep up the good work...
...wouldn't want to have to start *breaking* things.
P-please – be *careful!* Th-those are valuable prototypes! I...
...I'll do as you say.
BACK AT THE OFFICE...
Better get over to *Great Puttock,* stake out Bert Wall's house.
Mm. Weather's no better. Just as well I've got the Winter...
...Warmer!
Ee! It's *gone.* Some thieving tyke's *nicked* it!
Oh this is *not on!* Stealing an A.D.A.'s transportation in the middle of a case, that's... downright *criminal!*
Well I'm *not* chucking in the trilby just yet...

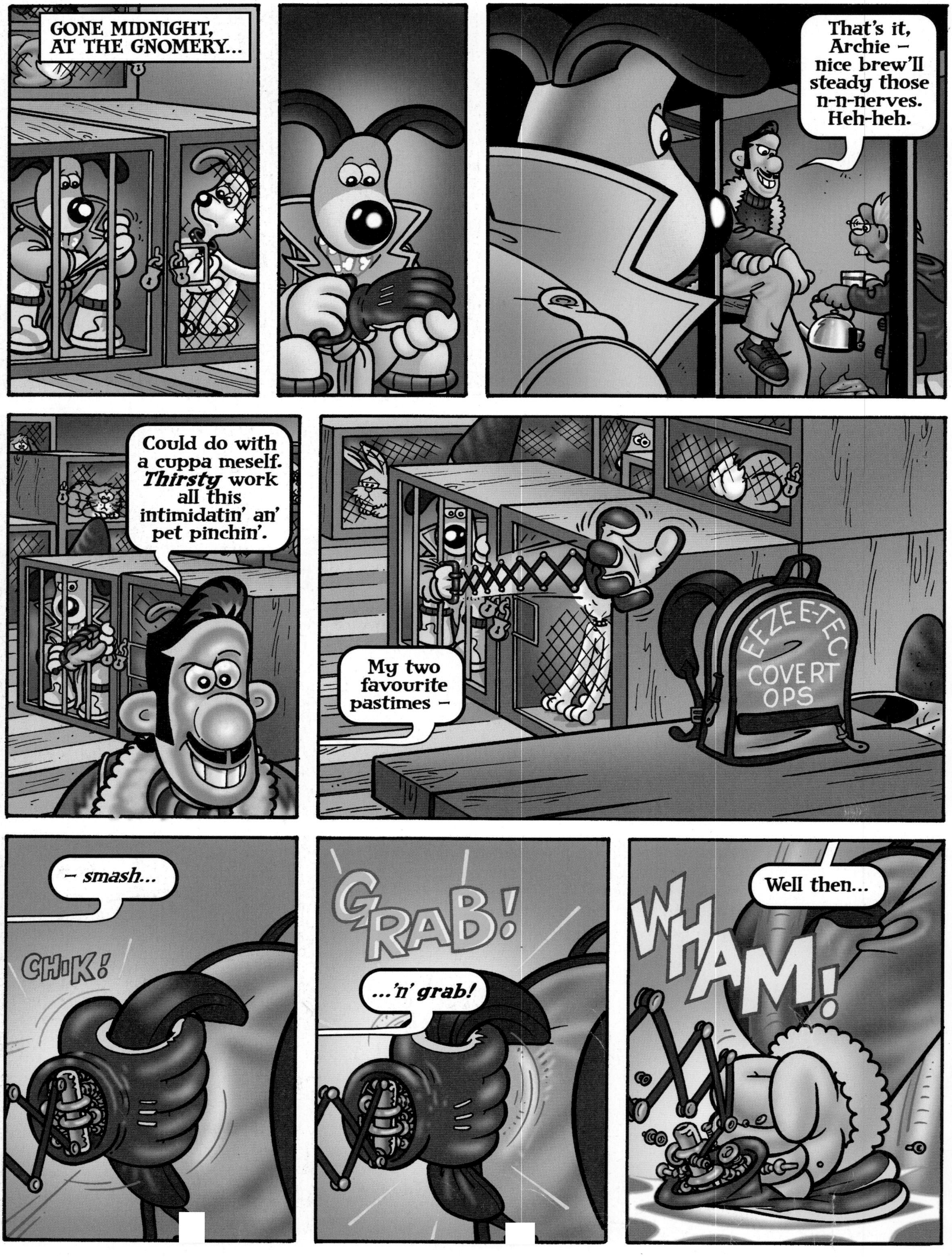
GONE MIDNIGHT, AT THE GNOMERY...
That's it, Archie – nice brew'll steady those n-n-nerves. Heh-heh.
Could do with a cuppa meself. *Thirsty* work all this intimidatin' an' pet pinchin'.
My two favourite pastimes –
EEZEE-TEC COVERT OPS
– smash...
CHIK!
GRAB!
...'n' grab!
Well then...
WHAM!

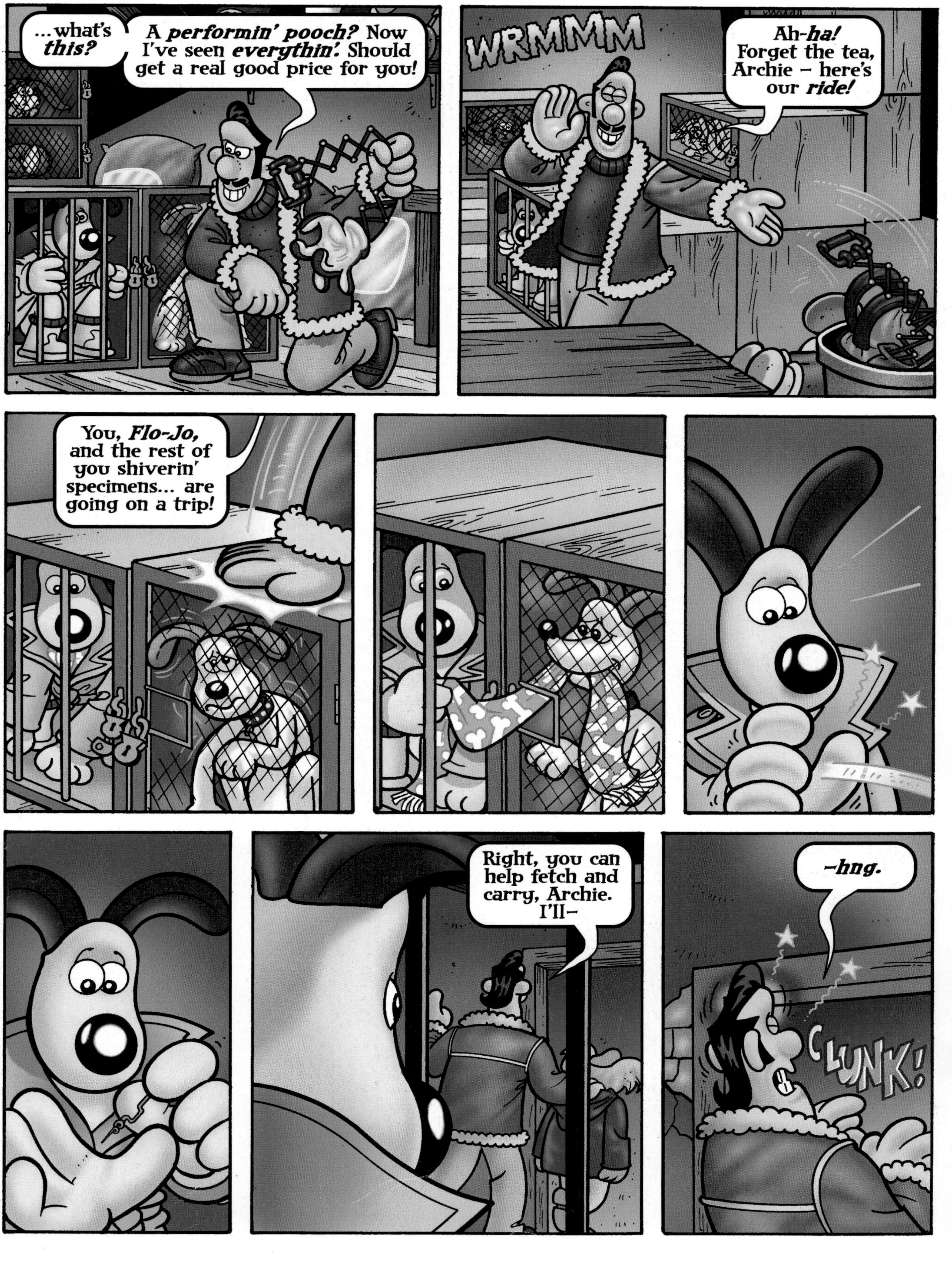

...what's this?
A performin' pooch? Now I've seen everythin'. Should get a real good price for you!
WRMMM
Ah-ha! Forget the tea, Archie – here's our ride!
You, Flo-Jo, and the rest of you shiverin' specimens... are going on a trip!
Right, you can help fetch and carry, Archie. I'll–
–hng.
CLUNK!

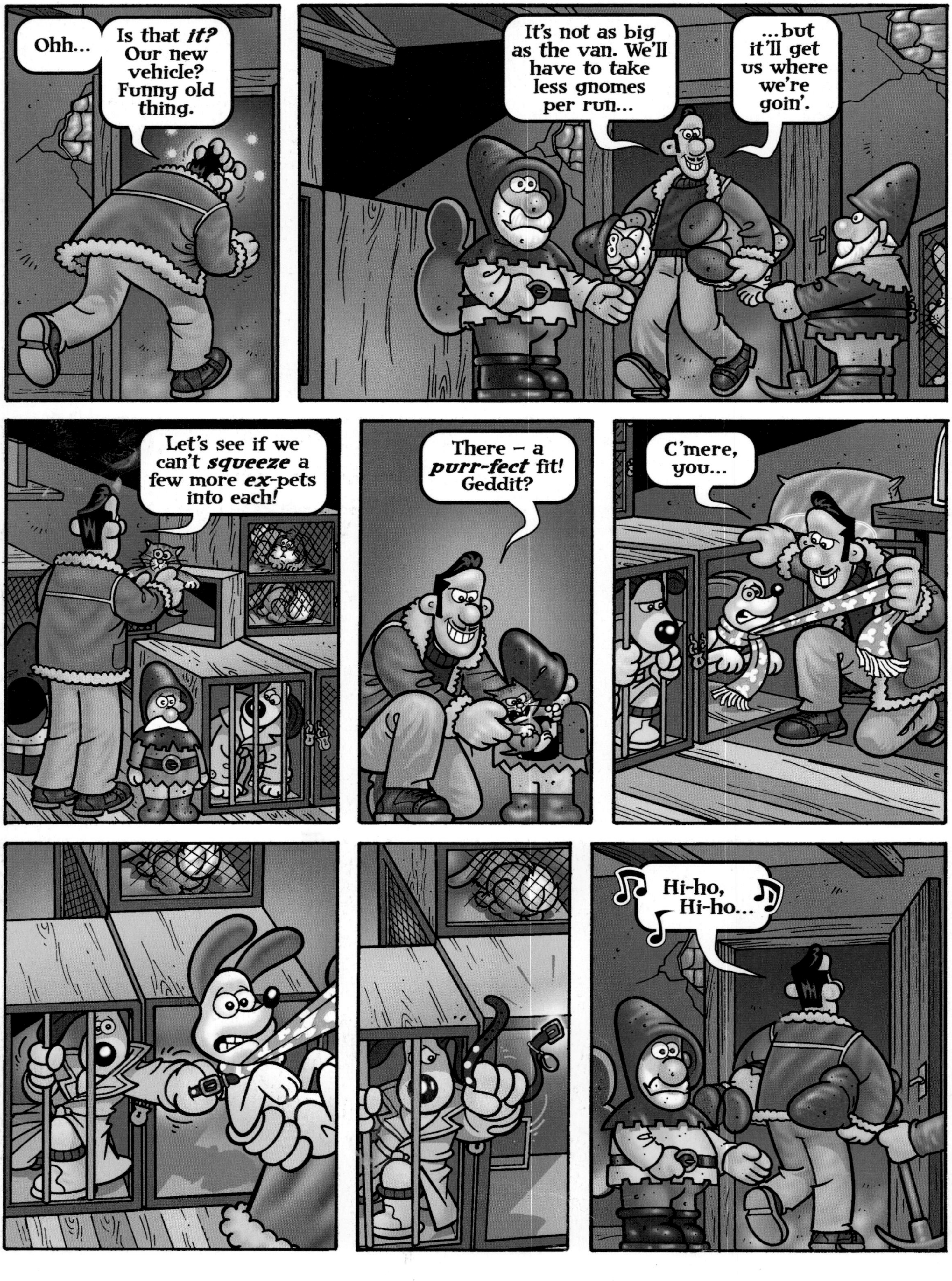
Ohh...
Is that *it?* Our new vehicle? Funny old thing.
It's not as big as the van. We'll have to take less gnomes per run...
...but it'll get us where we're goin'.
Let's see if we can't ***squeeze*** a few more ***ex***-pets into each!
There – a ***purr-fect*** fit! Geddit?
C'mere, you...
Hi-ho, Hi-ho...

WEST WALLABY STREET, THE EARLY HOURS...

There, *perfect!*

The *Sno-Blo, mark two*... is clear for launch!

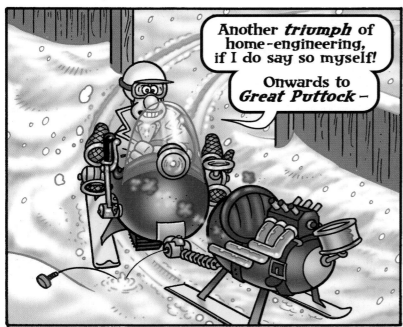

Another *triumph* of home-engineering, if I do say so myself!

Onwards to *Great Puttock* –

– and the *grand denouement!*

THE GNOMERY...

Okay, we're off. Be back later for the rest of you–uuh!

CLUNK!

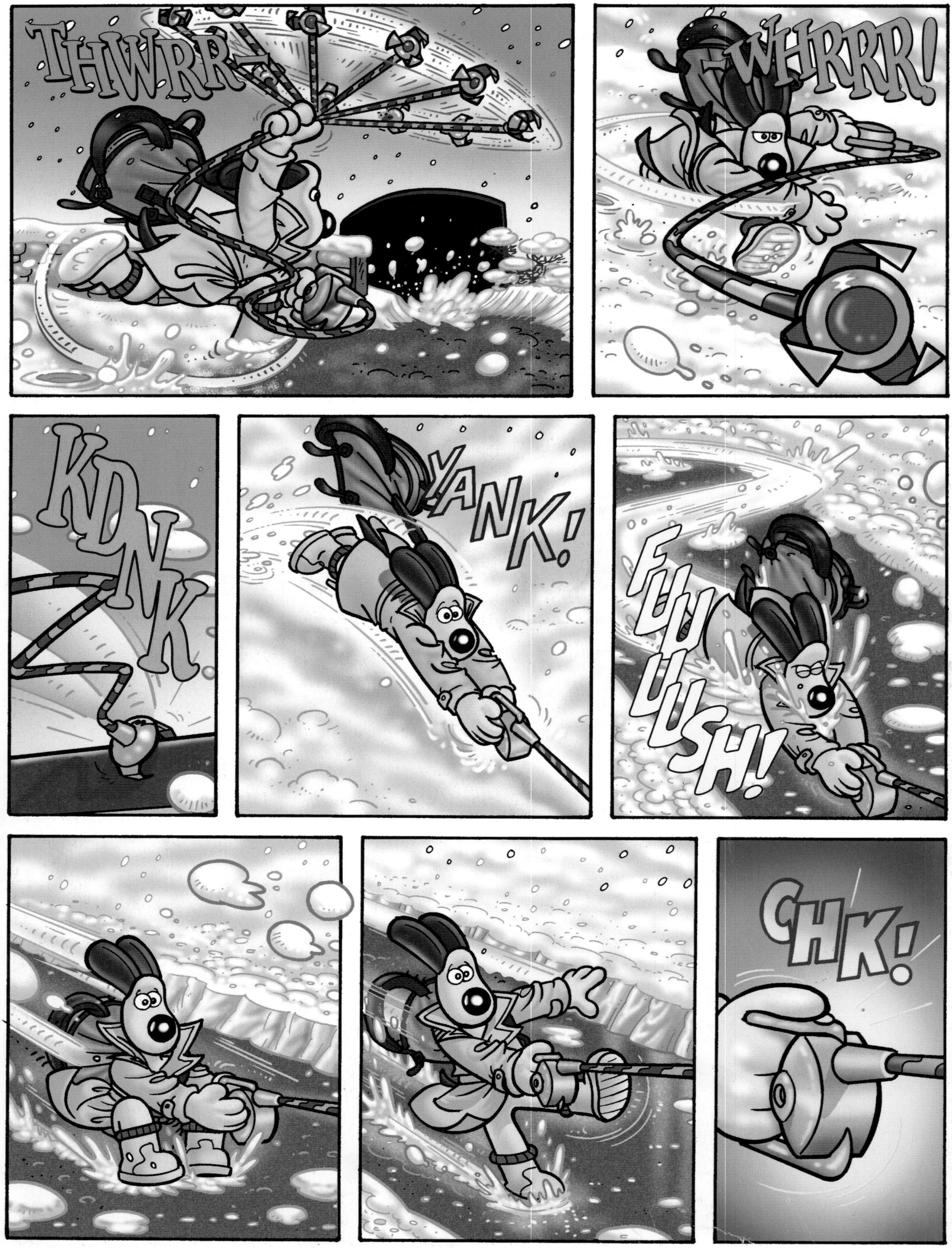
THHWRR–
–WHRRR!
KDNNK
YANK!
FUUUUUSH!
CHK!

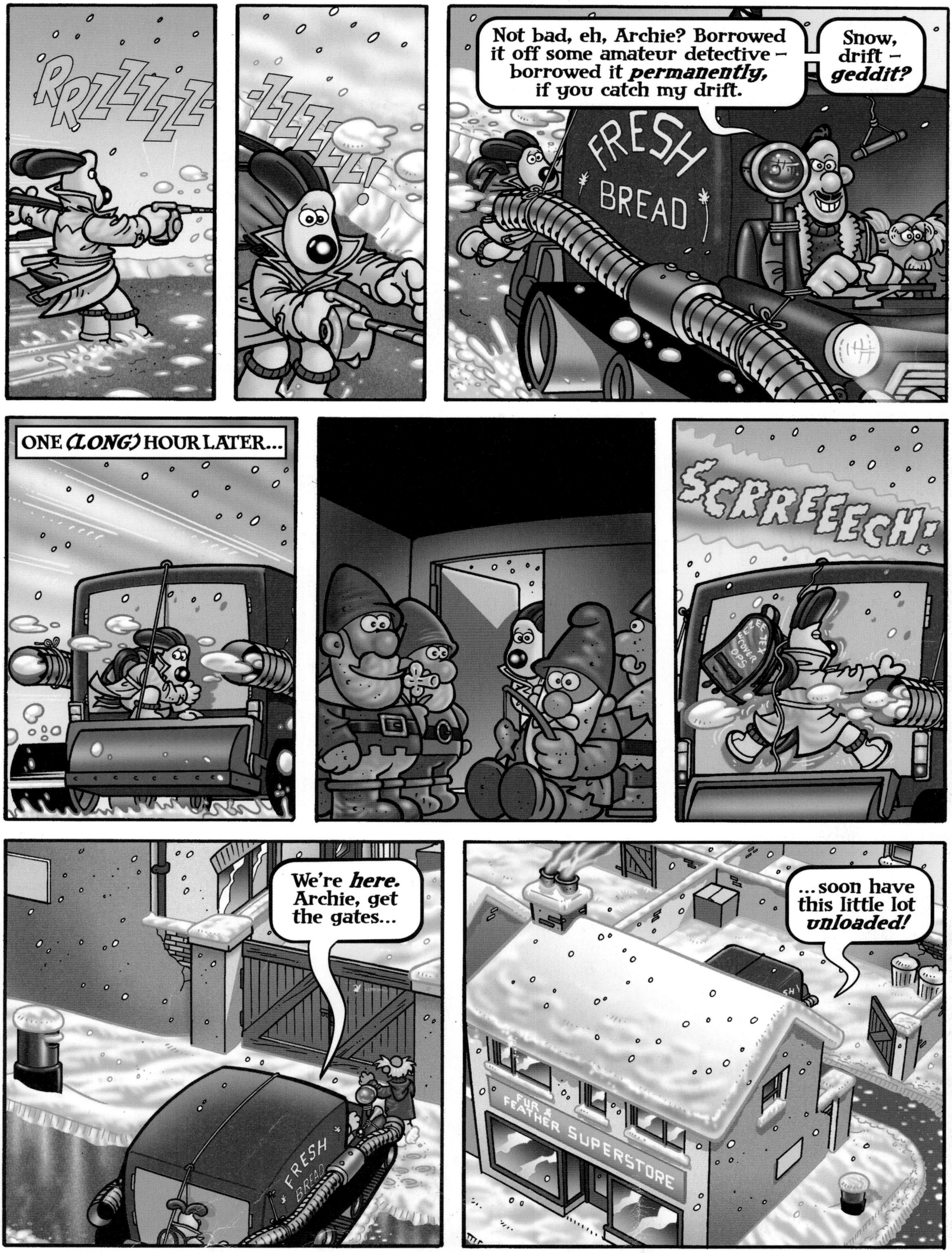
RRZZZZZZ-
-ZZZZLL!
Not bad, eh, Archie? Borrowed it off some amateur detective – borrowed it *permanently,* if you catch my drift.
Snow, drift – *geddit?*
FRESH BREAD
ONE *(LONG)* HOUR LATER...
SCRREEECH!
We're *here.* Archie, get the gates...
FRESH BREAD
...soon have this little lot *unloaded!*
FUR & FEATHER SUPERSTORE

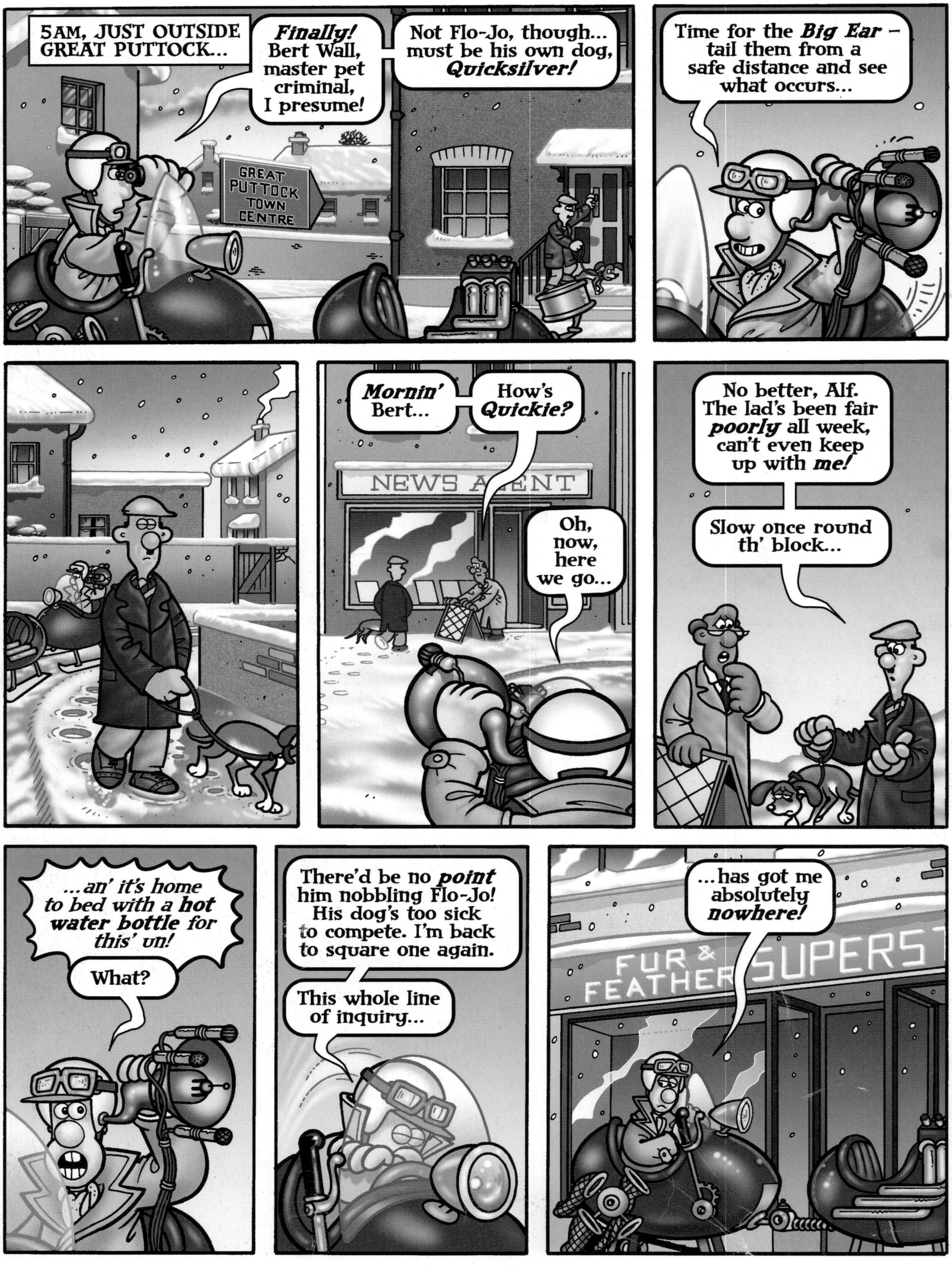
5AM, JUST OUTSIDE GREAT PUTTOCK...
Finally! Bert Wall, master pet criminal, I presume!
Not Flo-Jo, though... must be his own dog, Quicksilver!
GREAT PUTTOCK TOWN CENTRE
Time for the Big Ear – tail them from a safe distance and see what occurs...
Mornin' Bert...
How's Quickie?
NEWS AGENT
Oh, now, here we go...
No better, Alf. The lad's been fair poorly all week, can't even keep up with me!
Slow once round th' block...
...an' it's home to bed with a hot water bottle for this' un!
What?
There'd be no point him nobbling Flo-Jo! His dog's too sick to compete. I'm back to square one again.
This whole line of inquiry...
...has got me absolutely nowhere!
FUR & FEATHER SUPERST

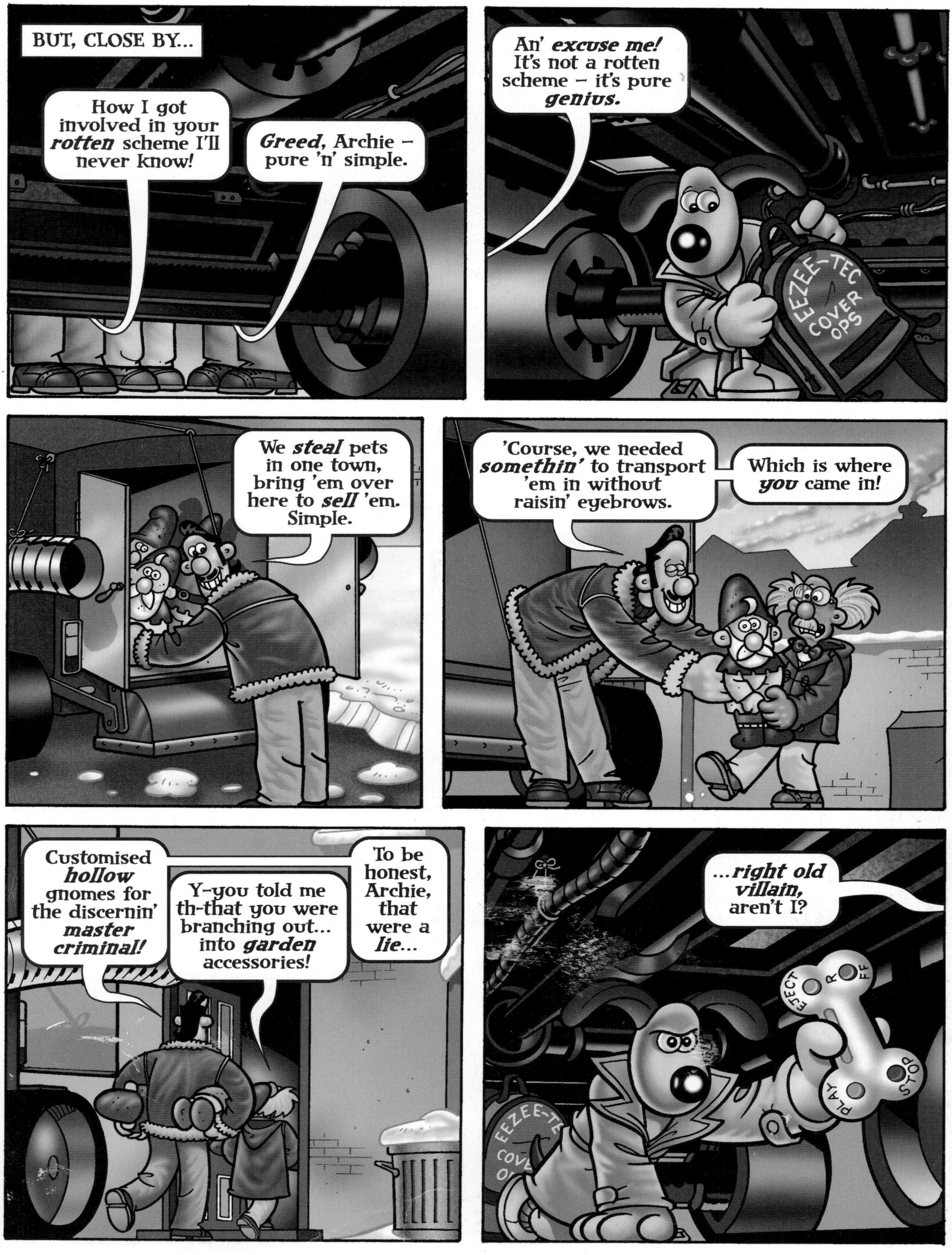
BUT, CLOSE BY...
How I got involved in your *rotten* scheme I'll never know!
Greed, Archie – pure 'n' simple.
An' *excuse me!* It's not a rotten scheme – it's pure *genius*.
EEZEE-TEC COVER OPS
We *steal* pets in one town, bring 'em over here to *sell* 'em. Simple.
'Course, we needed *somethin'* to transport 'em in without raisin' eyebrows.
Which is where *you* came in!
Customised *hollow* gnomes for the discernin' *master criminal!*
Y-you told me th-that you were branching out... into *garden* accessories!
To be honest, Archie, that were a *lie*...
...*right old villain,* aren't I?
EJECT R FF
PLAY STOP

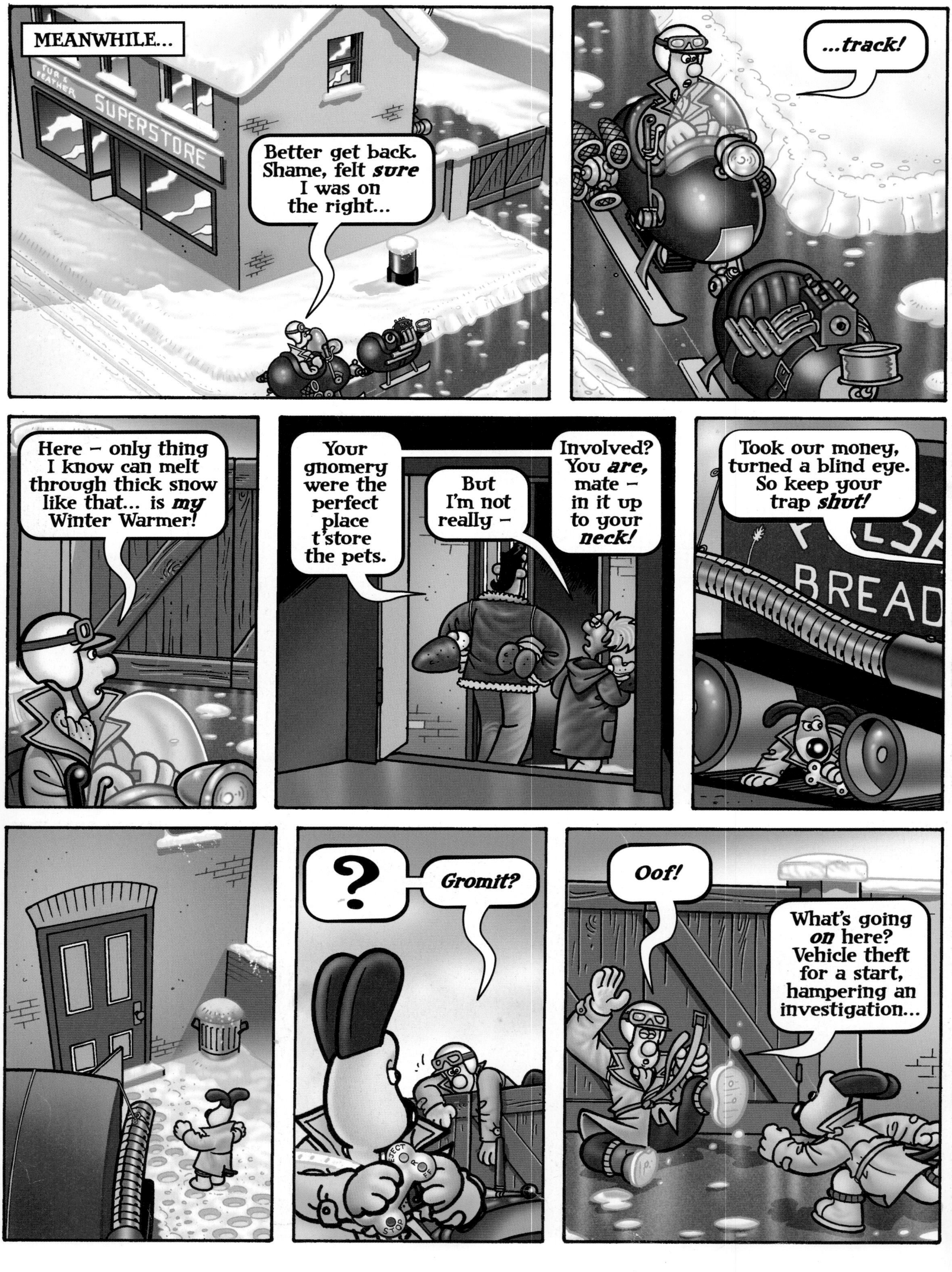
MEANWHILE...
FUR & FEATHER SUPERSTORE
Better get back. Shame, felt *sure* I was on the right...
...*track!*
Here – only thing I know can melt through thick snow like that... is *my* Winter Warmer!
Your gnomery were the perfect place t'store the pets.
But I'm not really –
Involved? You *are,* mate – in it up to your *neck!*
Took our money, turned a blind eye. So keep your trap *shut!*
BREAD
?
Gromit?
EJECT
STOP
Oof!
What's going *on* here? Vehicle theft for a start, hampering an investigation...

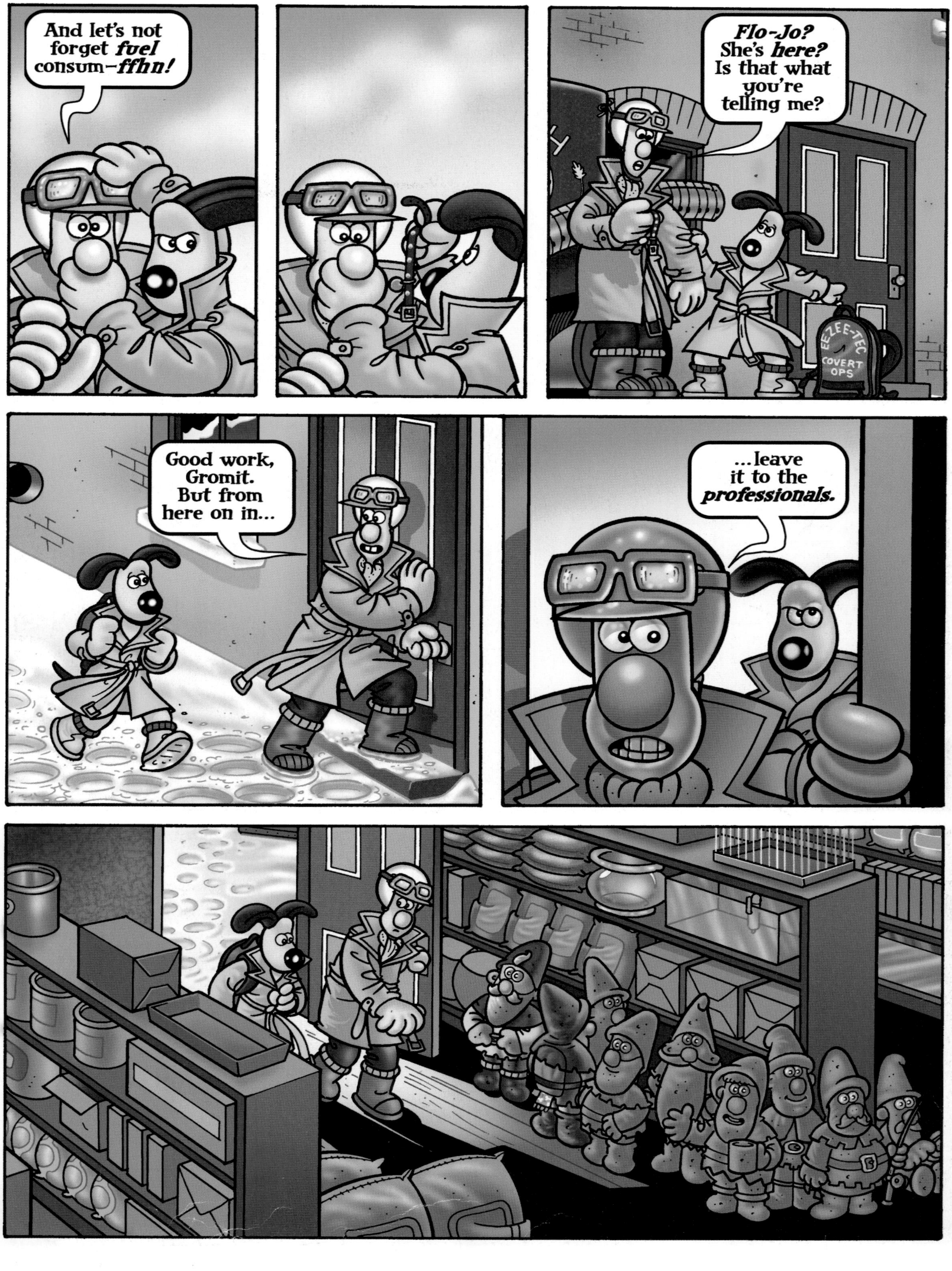

And let's not forget *fuel* consum-*ffhn!*
Flo-Jo? She's *here?* Is that what you're telling me?
EEZEE-TEC COVERT OPS
Good work, Gromit. But from here on in...
...leave it to the *professionals.*

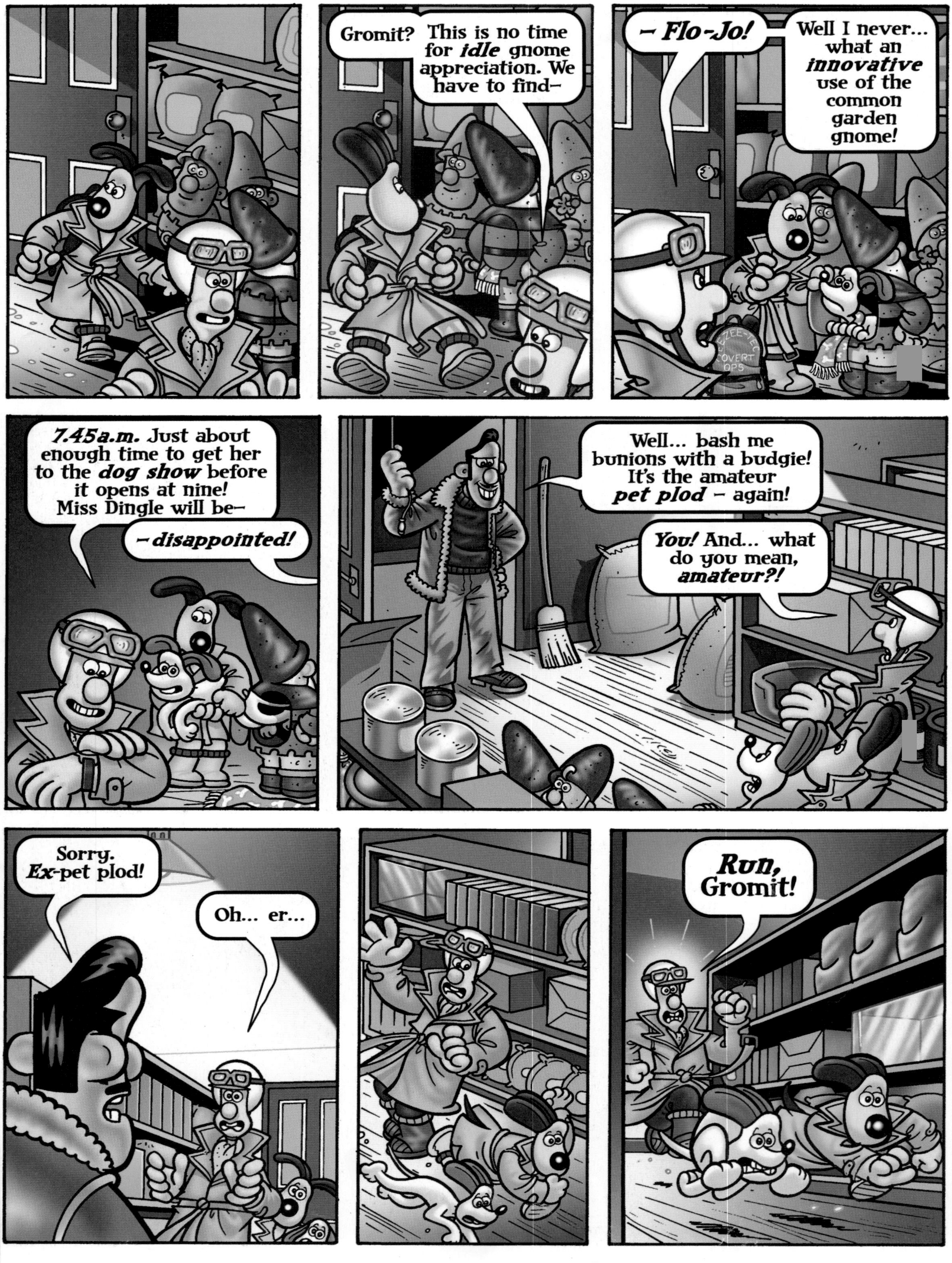

Gromit? This is no time for *idle* gnome appreciation. We have to find–
– *Flo-Jo!*
Well I never... what an *innovative* use of the common garden gnome!
COVERT OPS
7.45a.m. Just about enough time to get her to the *dog show* before it opens at nine! Miss Dingle will be–
– *disappointed!*
Well... bash me bunions with a budgie! It's the amateur *pet plod* – again!
You! And... what do you mean, *amateur?!*
Sorry. *Ex*-pet plod!
Oh... er...
Run, Gromit!

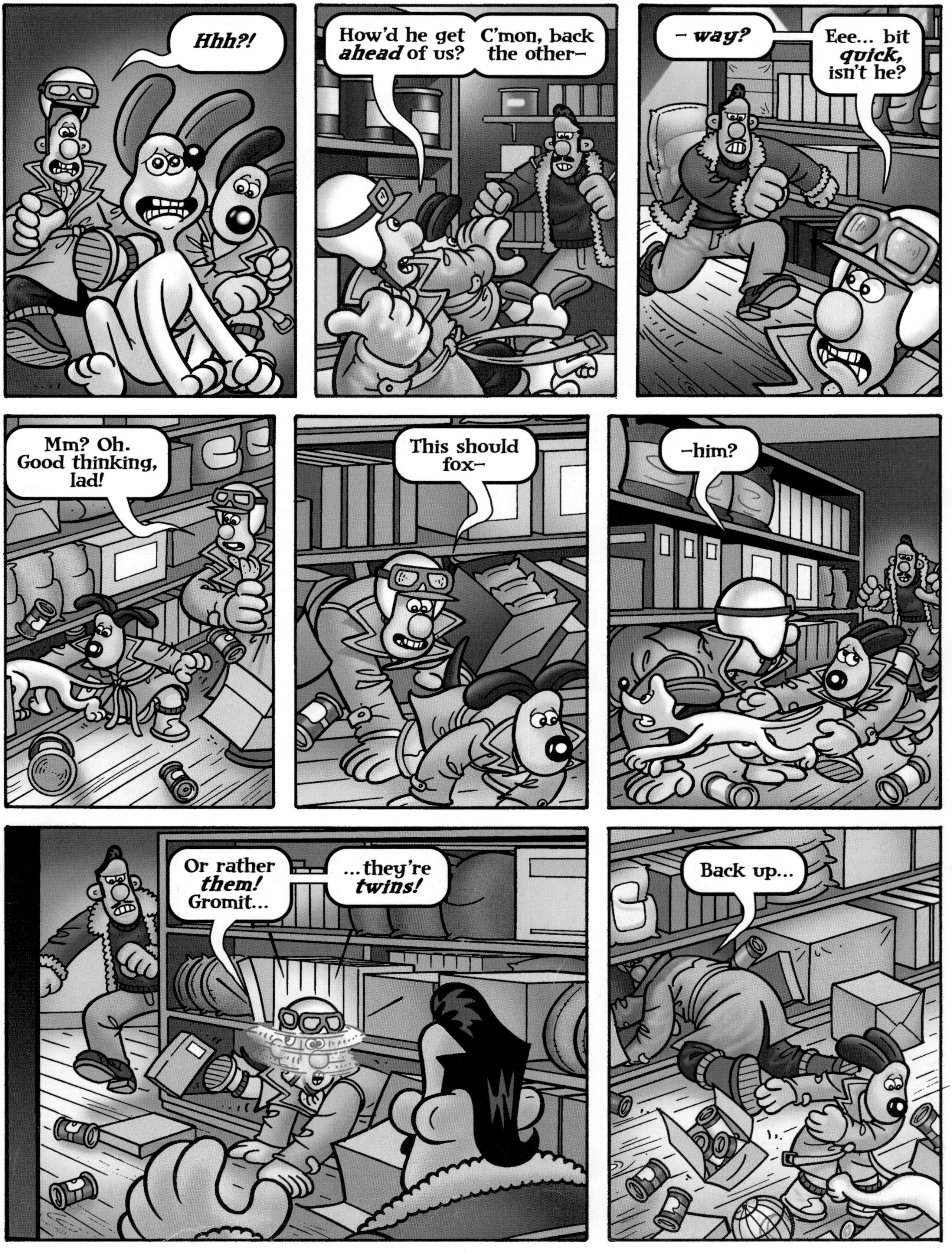
Hhh?!
How'd he get *ahead* of us?
C'mon, back the other–
– *way?*
Eee... bit *quick,* isn't he?
Mm? Oh. Good thinking, lad!
This should fox–
–him?
Or rather *them!* Gromit...
...they're *twins!*
Back up...

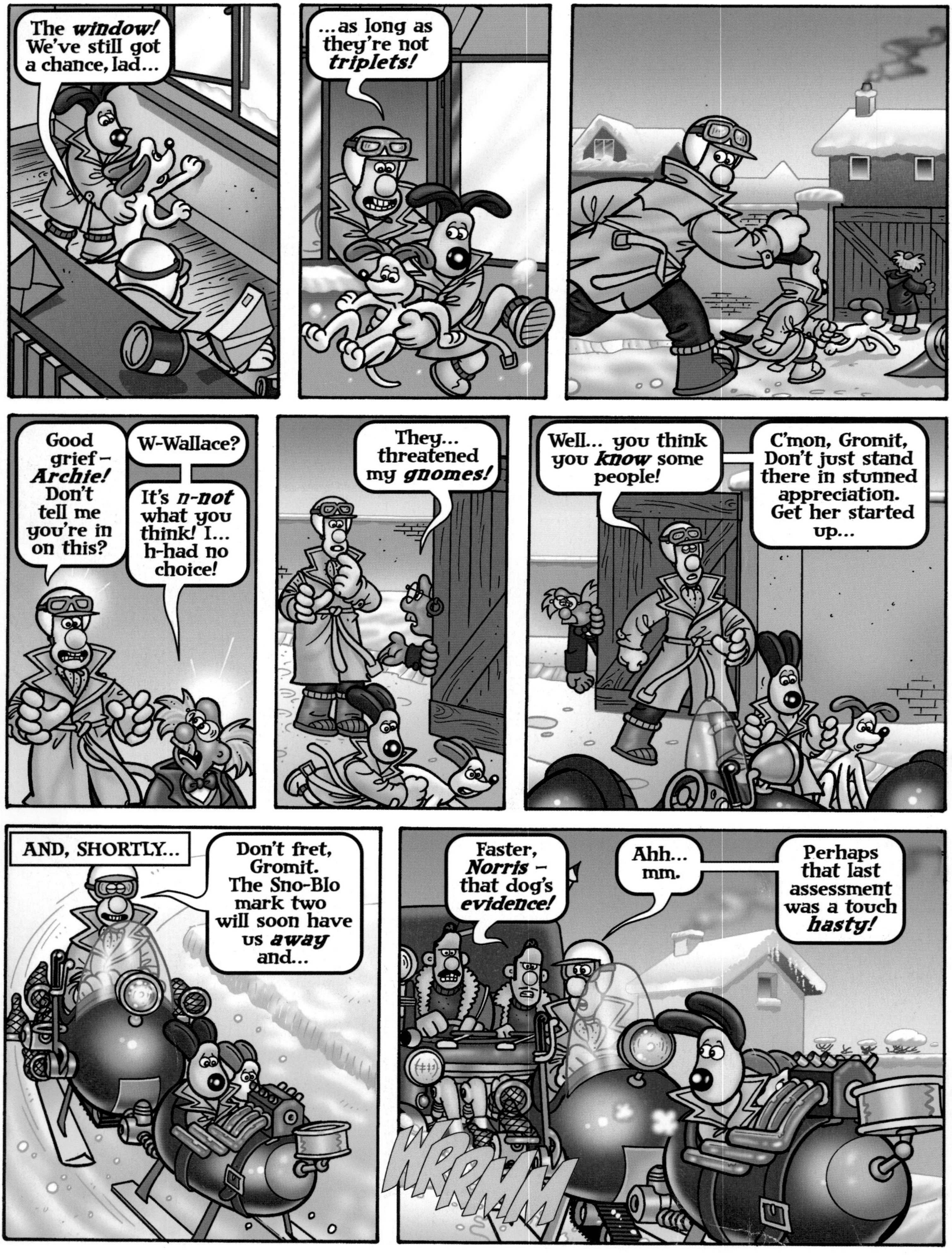
The *window!* We've still got a chance, lad...
...as long as they're not *triplets!*
Good grief – *Archie!* Don't tell me you're in on this?
W-Wallace?
It's *n-not* what you think! I... h-had no choice!
They... threatened my *gnomes!*
Well... you think you *know* some people!
C'mon, Gromit, Don't just stand there in stunned appreciation. Get her started up...
AND, SHORTLY...
Don't fret, Gromit. The Sno-Blo mark two will soon have us *away* and...
Faster, *Norris* – that dog's *evidence!*
Ahh... mm.
Perhaps that last assessment was a touch *hasty!*
WRRMM

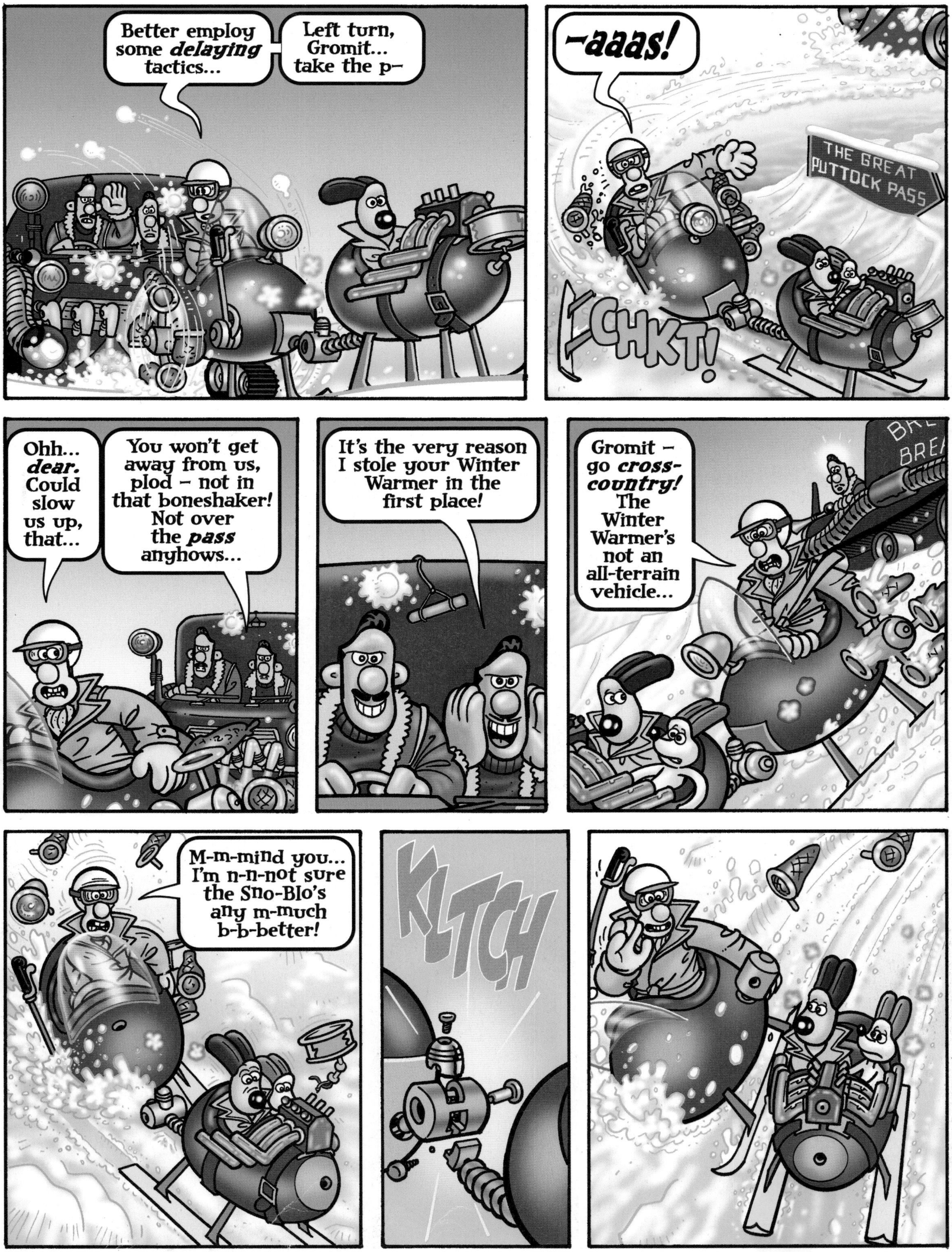
Better employ some *delaying* tactics...
Left turn, Gromit... take the p–
–aaas!
THE GREAT PUTTOCK PASS
CHKT!
Ohh... *dear.* Could slow us up, that...
You won't get away from us, plod – not in that boneshaker! Not over the *pass* anyhows...
It's the very reason I stole your Winter Warmer in the first place!
Gromit – go *cross-country!* The Winter Warmer's not an all-terrain vehicle...
M-m-mind you... I'm n-n-not sure the Sno-Blo's any m-much b-b-better!
KLTCH

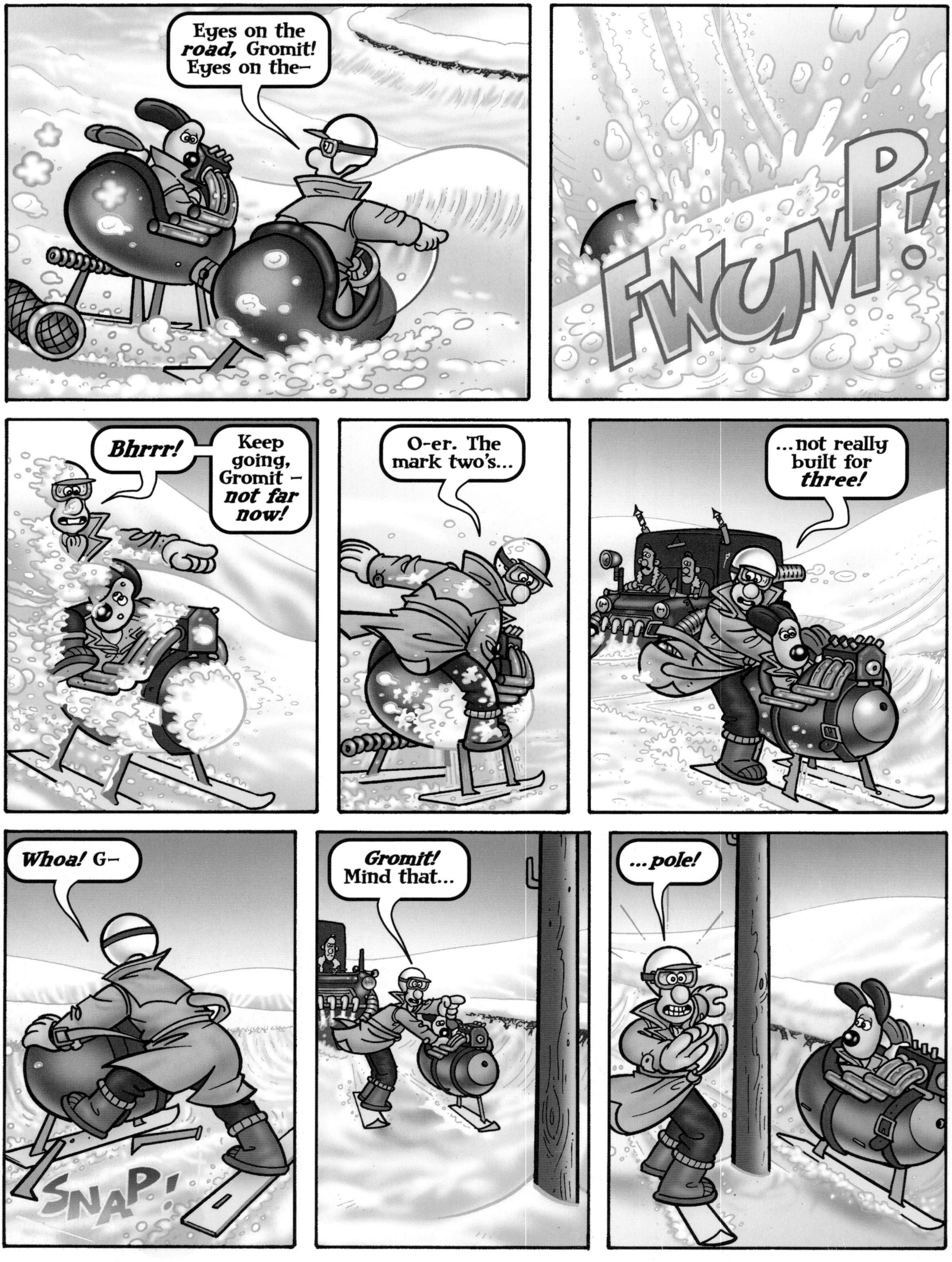
Eyes on the *road,* Gromit! Eyes on the–
FWUMP!
Bhrrr!
Keep going, Gromit – *not far now!*
O-er. The mark two's...
...not really built for *three!*
Whoa! G–
SNAP!
Gromit! Mind that...
...pole!

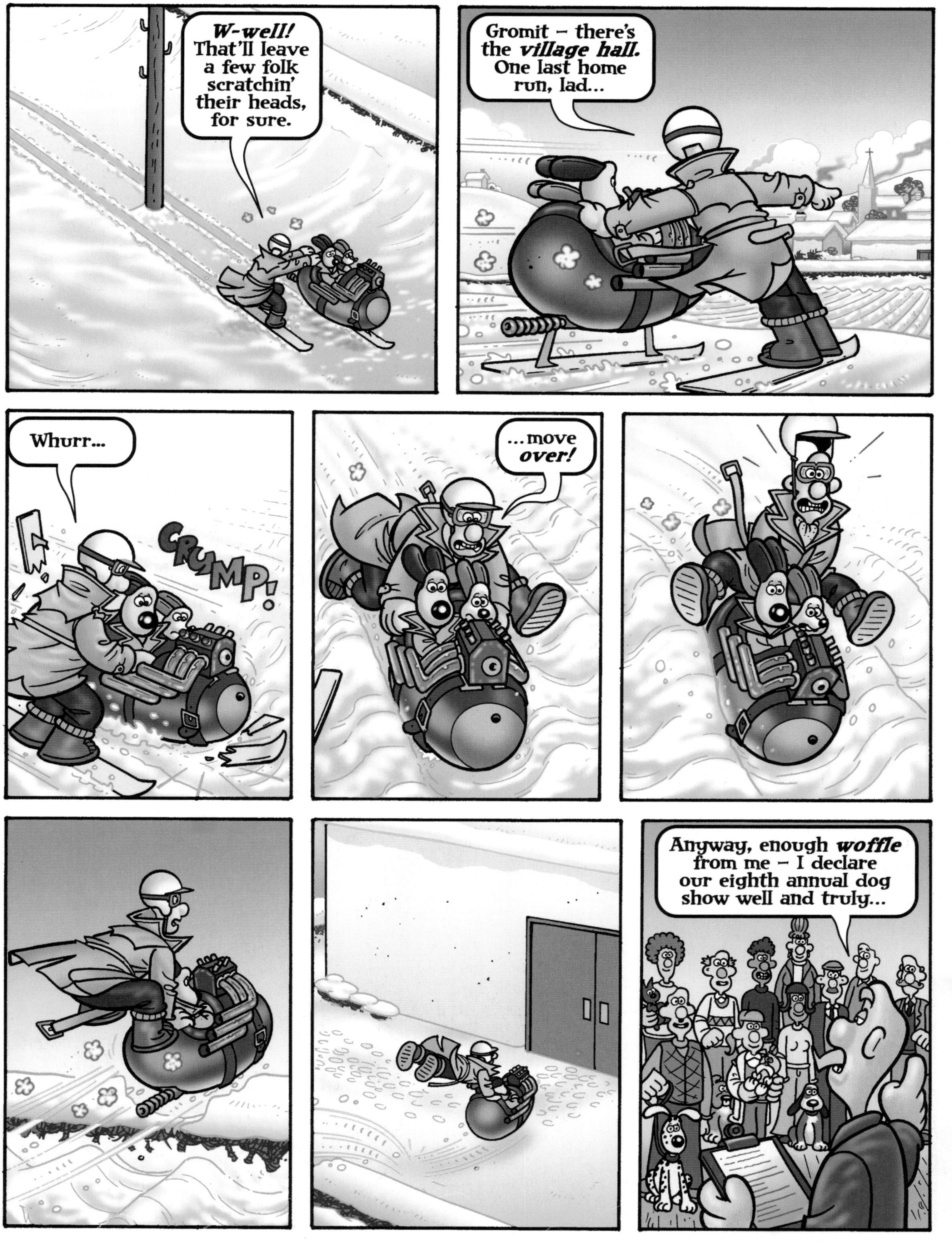
W-well! That'll leave a few folk scratchin' their heads, for sure.
Gromit – there's the village hall. One last home run, lad...
Whurr...
CRUMP!
...move over!
Anyway, enough woffle from me – I declare our eighth annual dog show well and truly...

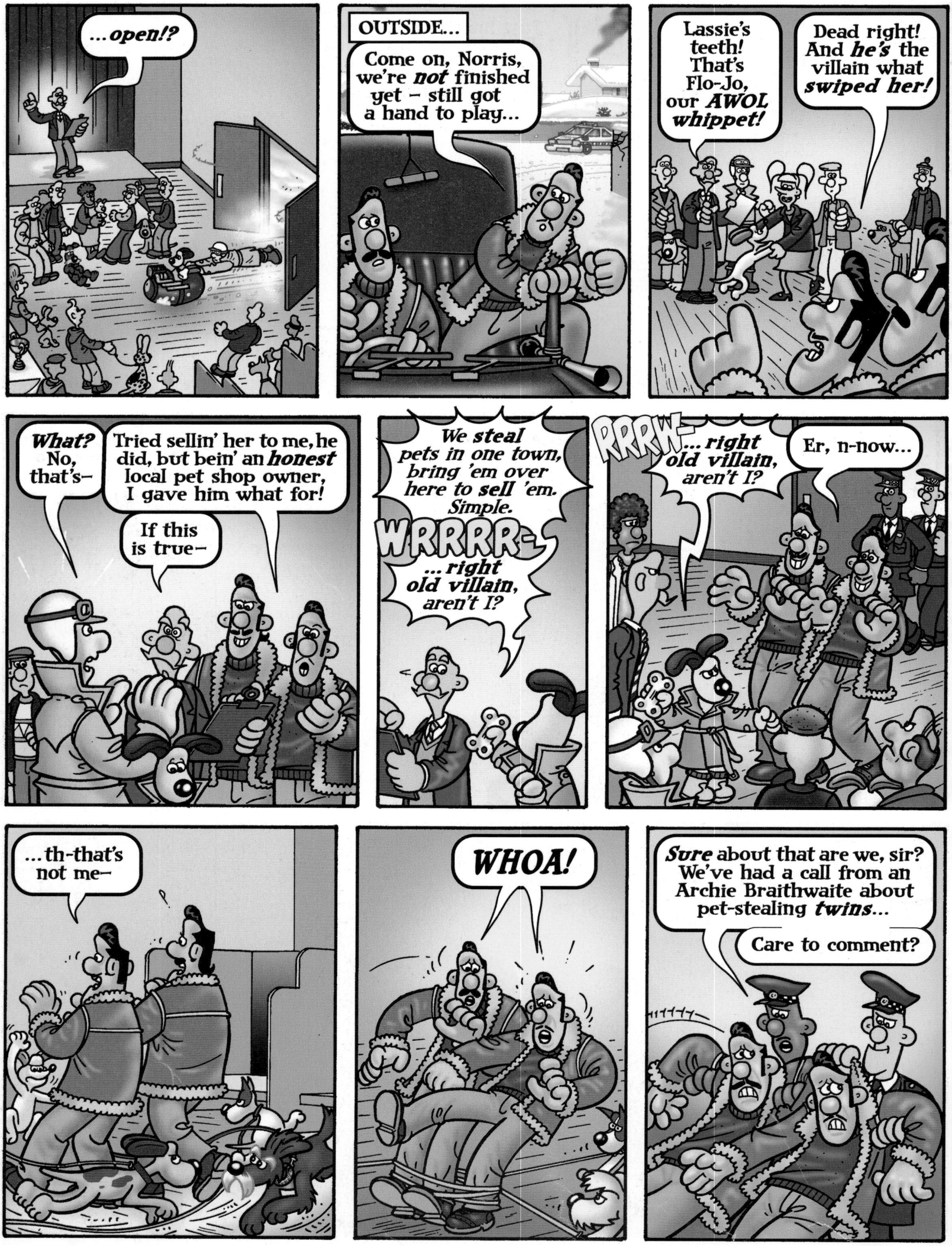

...open!?
OUTSIDE...
Come on, Norris, we're not finished yet – still got a hand to play...
Lassie's teeth! That's Flo-Jo, our AWOL whippet!
Dead right! And he's the villain what swiped her!
What? No, that's–
Tried sellin' her to me, he did, but bein' an honest local pet shop owner, I gave him what for!
If this is true–
We steal pets in one town, bring 'em over here to sell 'em. Simple.
WRRRR–
...right old villain, aren't I?
RRRW–
...right old villain, aren't I?
Er, n-now...
...th-that's not me–
WHOA!
Sure about that are we, sir? We've had a call from an Archie Braithwaite about pet-stealing twins...
Care to comment?

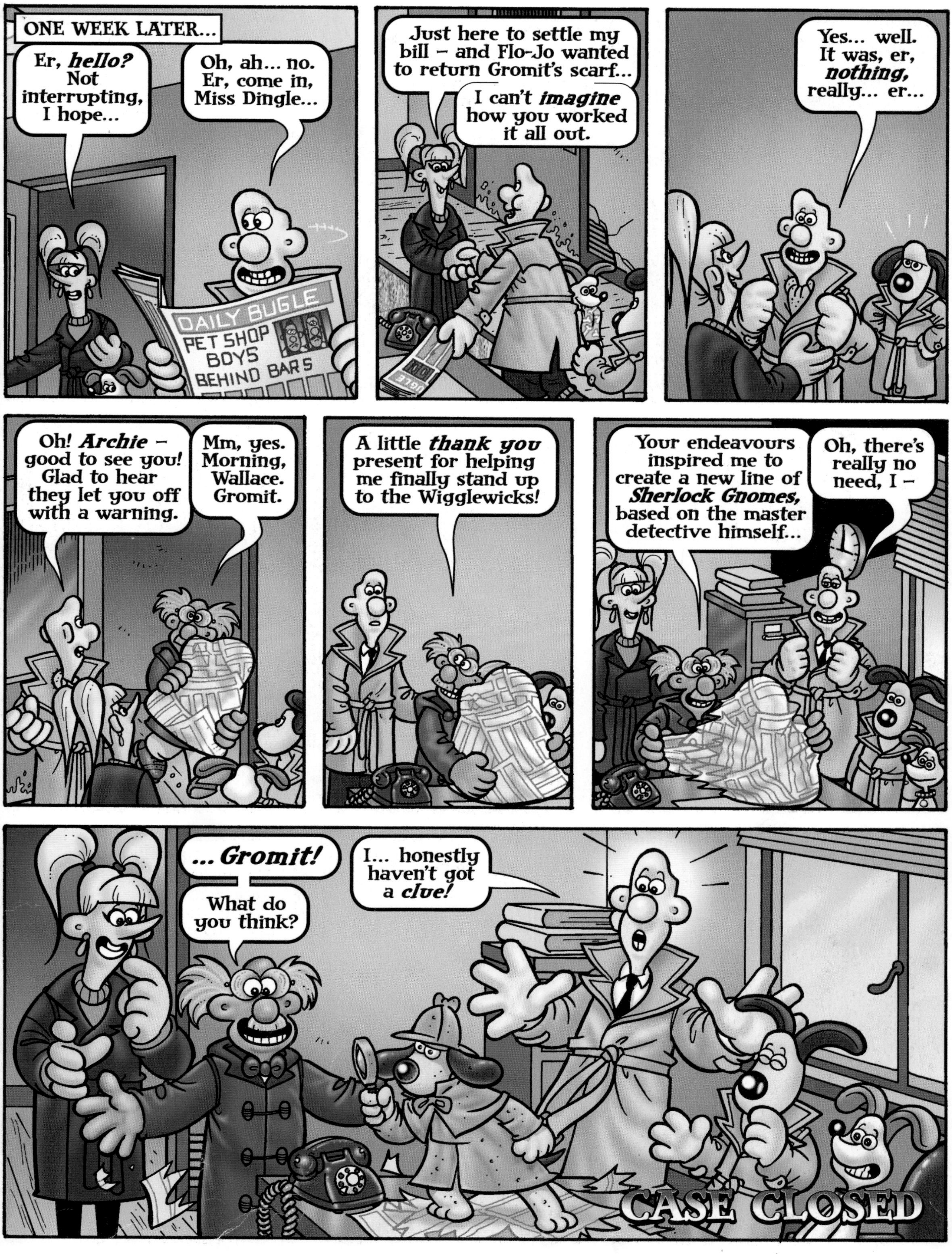
ONE WEEK LATER...
Er, *hello?* Not interrupting, I hope...
Oh, ah... no. Er, come in, Miss Dingle...
DAILY BUGLE
PET SHOP BOYS BEHIND BARS
Just here to settle my bill – and Flo-Jo wanted to return Gromit's scarf...
I can't *imagine* how you worked it all out.
Yes... well. It was, er, *nothing,* really... er...
Oh! *Archie* – good to see you! Glad to hear they let you off with a warning.
Mm, yes. Morning, Wallace. Gromit.
A little *thank you* present for helping me finally stand up to the Wigglewicks!
Your endeavours inspired me to create a new line of *Sherlock Gnomes,* based on the master detective himself...
Oh, there's really no need, I –
...Gromit!
What do you think?
I... honestly haven't got a *clue!*
CASE CLOSED

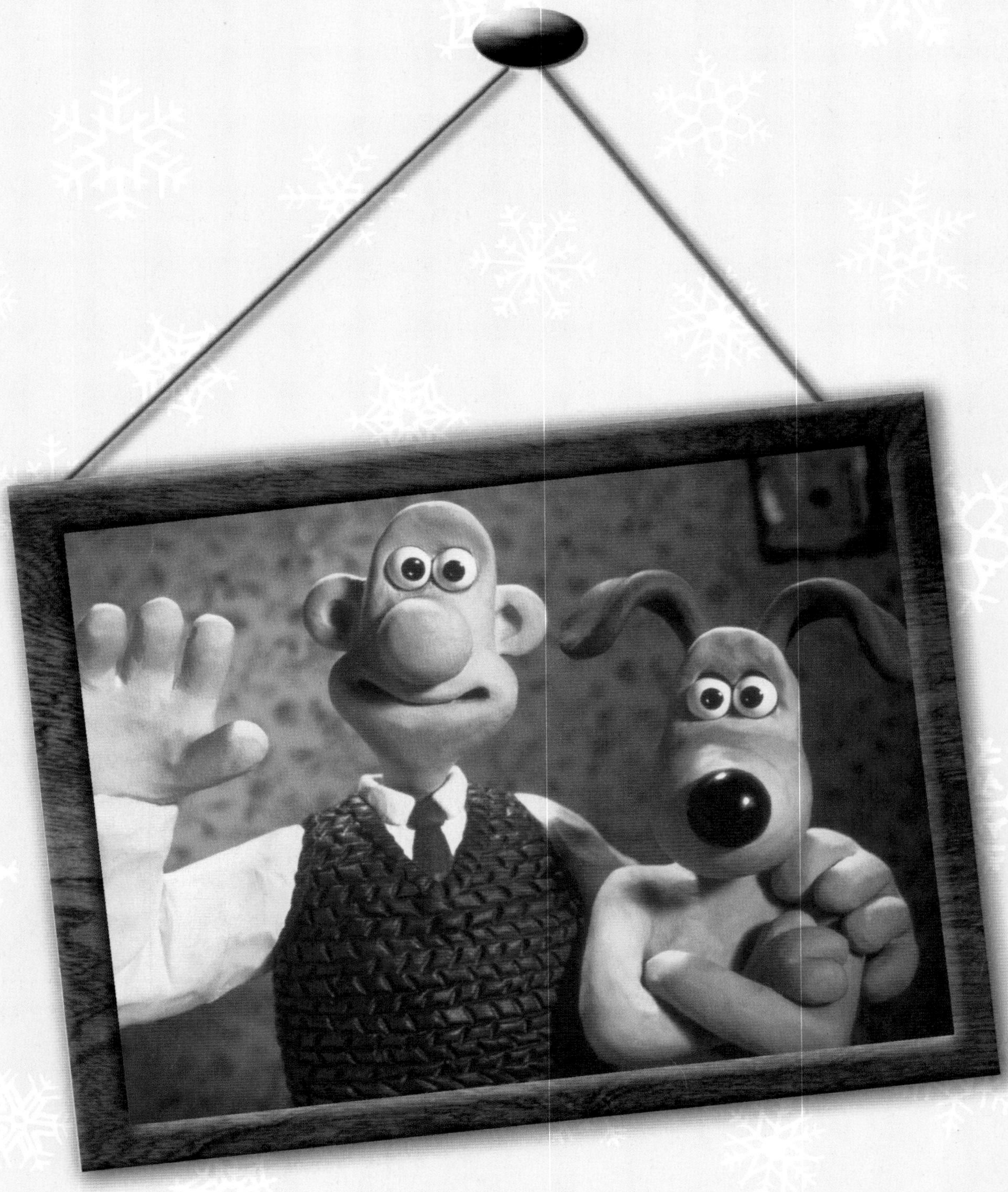

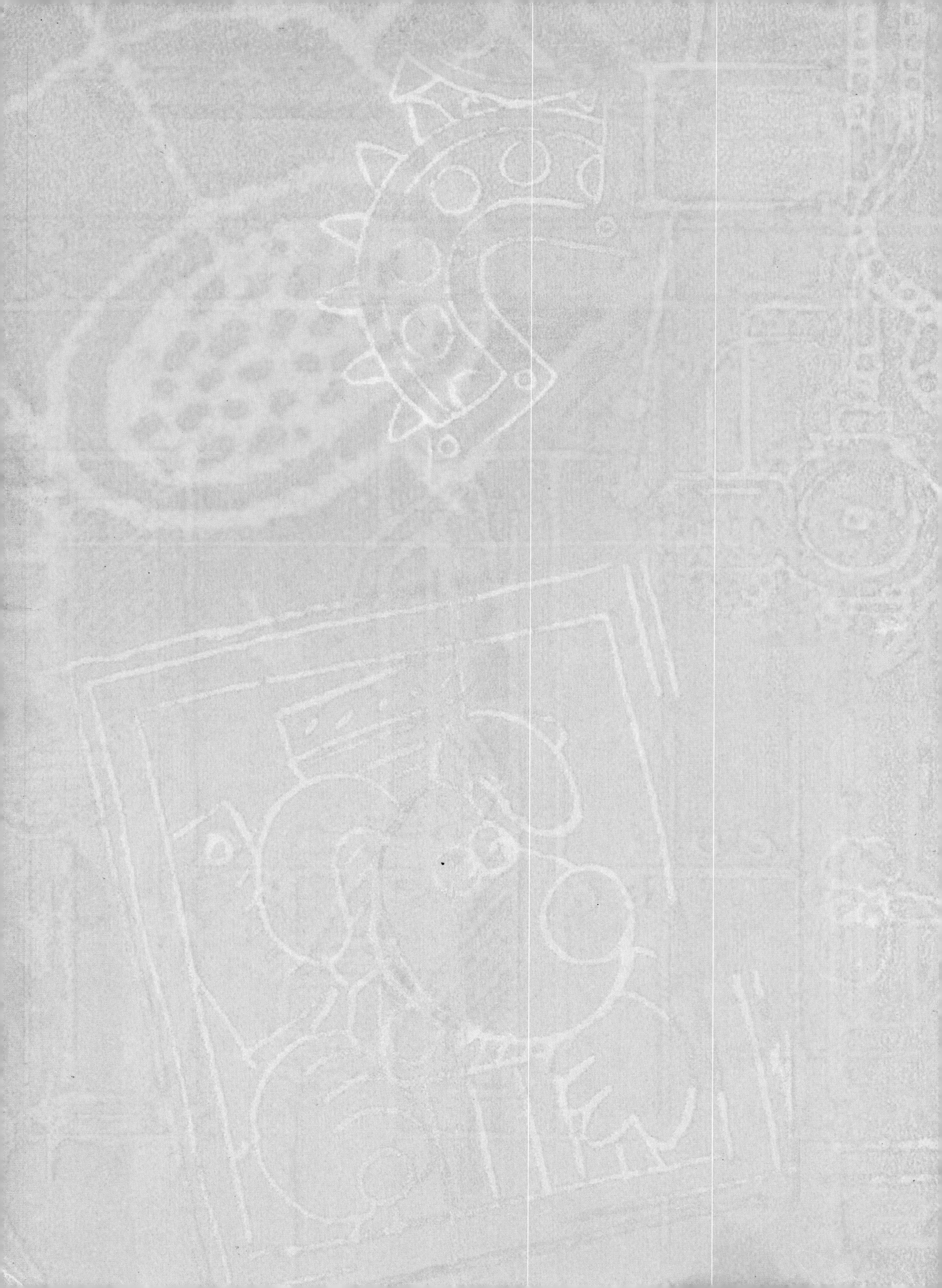